Shedding

Lies

Living Beyond
Childhood Trauma

DR. ANNE KATONA LINN

You can only truly experience joy once you have grieved.

I used to think I could only be happy if I could get rid of my childhood baggage.

Having an awareness of trauma helped me get through the COVID-19 pandemic.
—David Lee, Lifeline Association Co-Founder at Pennsylvania State Correctional Institute at Coal Township

Download Your Free Classroom Guide!

To thank you for purchasing my book,
download my free guide:

**Three Ultimate Strategies to Quiet the
Stress Storm in Your Classroom**

Decrease stress in the classroom and
create a positive school climate.

Scan the QR code below:

Or visit the link below:

bit.ly/3gg2sU7

table of Contents

Introduction

I am a Gen X, latch-key kid, the seventh child in a family of baby boomers. I was born eight years after my youngest sibling in the family when my parents were thirty-nine years old. I know I was not planned, and at times felt that I wasn't wanted; my dad was finished raising kids by the time I came along. Eight years are between the oldest and the next youngest sibling. Four girls and three boys. People always asked me, "Are you Catholic or Mormon?" We were a big Catholic family growing up in small-town Pennsylvania to first-generation Eastern European parents who were the youngest in their families.

Our parents were not wealthy in any way, and my parents lived in Dad's parent's house when they were first married. Yet we were a very respected family. Others looked up to us as a "good family," and we all had good reputations as good athletes, students, friends, children, and Catholics.

I grew up in a four-bedroom house that we thought was a palace. I always thought we were upper middle class because we had a single-family home with a big yard. My dad had several jobs over the lifespan of my siblings' childhoods as an insurance salesperson, Heinz ketchup salesman, and finally, a US Postal Carrier during my childhood. My mom was a stay-at-home mom raising six kids before I was born. It must have been challenging, having six children under eight years old. Their highest combined income was $28,000 in 1984. I know that because I had to write it down on the FAFSA application for college student loans. We never thought we were poor, but I know that money was a luxury.

I grew up in a small town in Central Pennsylvania that was a scene from the *Wonder Years*. It was 1966, and my parents already had six children between the ages of eight and sixteen. My mom was a short woman who had a personality like Mother Teresa. Everyone loved her, and she was everyone's "mom." Most kids in our neighborhood knew her as girl scout leader, babysitter, gym teacher's aide, swim teacher, or swim coach. By the time I came around, she was an aide to a reading specialist and librarian at the local elementary school. My mom was a powerhouse in a small package and helped thousands of children and adults learn to swim and be better human beings by her example.

My mom grew up as the youngest of six siblings in the town next to where our family lived. She had three brothers and one sister who was sixteen years older. We had lots of cousins and a very close-knit family. My mom was nineteen years old when her mother was hit by a truck and killed. She was on her way home after visiting family in the Scranton area. She didn't talk about it a lot, but I could not imagine the pain of losing her mom at a young age.

Her older sister, Helen, became her "mom" as Helen was sixteen years older than my mom. Her four older brothers were a little overbearing. They thought they knew better than her and freely shared their opinions, as older brothers often do. Their dad, my grandfather, owned a beer distributor in town. His son's brothers worked in the business along with their oldest sister, Helen. My mom sold her stock in the business when she got married. She did not want to be under the thumb of her older brothers. She always had a little bit of rebelliousness in her. My dad was not pleased about that. Because financially, her shares in the family business could have really helped, especially since she and dad had so many children. My mom's parents died long before I was born, so I never knew them.

My dad grew up in the same hometown where we grew up. He was a dapper dresser and had the most extensive record collection in town, earning him the nickname of the town disc jockey. His siblings were an older brother and a sister. They died in their forties, so I didn't know either of them very well. I later found out my dad's family experienced multiple traumas. I wondered if this contributed to them dying at such an early age. My father's parents owned a grocery store in town.

My dad was in the Navy, and he signed up at the age of seventeen. Because of this, he had to get his dad to sign off because he was not of legal age. So, he enlisted in the Navy during World War Two and was stationed in Guam. He did not tell many stories about his experiences during the war, and I wondered about the war's effect on him later in life. His sister, Aunt Tootsie, wrote back and forth to our dad during the war, and Dad kept the letters. We found letters when we cleaned their house after mom ended up in the nursing home. One of our cousins took the letters since Aunt Tootsie was her grandmother. So, she researched and authored a book about *Gibbs and Toots,* largely focused on the letters they wrote back and forth. It is hard to know what he thought because we don't have letters that he wrote to her, and from what we gather, he didn't write very often.

I was a beautiful child with blonde hair and golden brown-green eyes. I was athletic, intelligent, and popular with our neighborhood and school kids. Our community was close-knit, and everyone knew each other's business. Our town was like the Ozzy and Harriet version of a community, though we did not all have the money they had. The adage, "It takes a village," perfectly represents how children in the community were raised.

I forgive myself for buying into the lie that my parents and siblings did not want me. The truth is that even though I was unexpected, I was loved. They did the best they could with what they received themselves. It was a sign of the times.

Chapter 1

Early Memories—You Are Not Worthy

I do not remember a lot before the age of four. I had many different people watching me as my mom worked. I have this deep-seated feeling of abandonment because I did not have one person that I bonded with at that early age. So, I bonded with many people, and I feel like that created a gap for me.

My dad did not take care of me, as that was not the man's role back in the late 1960s. My mom was always my safe person, though she didn't have the time to give me much attention. She took me to work, but I had to share her with hundreds of other kids.

Growing up, I looked at my siblings and wanted to be like them. My relationships with my siblings often felt like I was begging for their attention. They would take me to different events with them, yet I always felt like I was an annoyance rather than a welcome companion. They may not have expressed their disdain for me directly, but I felt that disdain during most of my childhood and into young adulthood.

The actions of the adults in my life at this early stage gave me a feeling that I was an afterthought. I felt like I was a bother to them, even at that age. No one wanted to be raising a baby and toddler at that point in their lives. I felt like a doll people wanted to carry around and put down when they did not want to deal with me anymore.

I know that my family did not intend to make me feel rejected. It was part of the culture in the late sixties, and they didn't know anything different. They did not know that their behaviors affected me deeply. Unspoken words and actions impact young children more than we realize. Even though this period was relatively short, it showed me how critical those early years are for child development. The concept of "serve and return" interactions between primary caregivers and young children sets the foundation for lifelong relationships and functioning.

1970's—The Car Accident

One of my very first memories as a child was of violence. It was a summer day in 1970 when I was four years old. I went with my parents and seventeen-year-old sister to drop off something for my oldest sister at nursing school. She was having an event at school, and we were bringing her a dress.

I remember being in the car, excited to wear my favorite sailor-girl outfit. It was a little onesie with bloomer legs, and it was sleeveless with a white collar. I was excited to show my sister the outfit. We were on a busy highway in Allentown, Pennsylvania. Route 22 is usually a hectic road, and it was extra busy that day. A garbage truck on the side of the road lost some stuff and created a traffic jam.

I was sleeping and woke up when we stopped in traffic. It was about to storm, and I was afraid. I do not know if thunderstorms frightened me before the accident or not. I know that they became a massive trigger for me after the accident. As it started to rain, I went to the front seat, which was already full. I sat on my mom's lap next to the passenger door in the front seat. 1970, child safety laws did not yet exist, and cars had bench seats and no seat belts.

My dad was driving, and my middle sister, Trish, was in the middle of the front bench seat. We suddenly stopped, and our car slammed into the back of the car in front of us. My face hit the windshield first with the full force of my unrestricted tiny body. I do not remember this exact moment, but I probably was knocked out by the impact of my head on the windshield.

I remember all the other accident details more than fifty years later. I significantly damaged my face, and I was bleeding heavily. My mom took me out of the car, and an off-duty police officer stopped to help. He gave my mom the shirt off his back to stop the bleeding, then drove us to the hospital. My mom was using the man's shirt to put pressure on the wounds on my face. The area above my left eye had the most severe damage, with a large slice in the skin that now wanted to hang down over my eye. She had to press that piece of skin back to my forehead and hold it there. I remember telling my mom to stop pressing so hard, but she said she had to so I would not lose too much blood. That memory is vivid to this day, more than fifty years later. I remember the pressure on my face, the pain, the sounds of the car, and the feeling of my mom trying to comfort me. It was all unsure as I was in and out of consciousness during the drive.

I do not remember who, but someone carried me into the emergency room at Sacred Heart Hospital in Allentown. When we got inside, I remember the doctors and nurses pulling me away from my parents and sister. That instance is seared in my memory for life. Terror ran through my little, blood-covered body. I was crying loudly and trying to hold onto my parents because I did not know what was happening. Why would someone take me away from them and not let them stay with me? I cannot even imagine what that felt like for my family. The questions that ran through my head were, "Why didn't they fight for me? What did I do to deserve this punishment?" Later in life, my mom told me that my sister Trish went into shock when she saw my injuries. Yes, I suffered physical injuries, but the emotional trauma must have been harrowing for my parents and sister to deal with. Yet it wasn't until years later that I learned they were traumatized by the event. For years I did not know they were affected because we didn't talk about it, and they felt they needed to be strong for me.

Now that I have four young granddaughters, I cannot imagine having to "give them up" for *any* reason to doctors and nurses without a fight. My experiences kick my mama bear brain into fight mode because I vividly remember my experiences. Not only is the threat of separation a horrible thought but witnessing a young child in pain and in uncertain situations is still a trigger for me to this day.

I woke up in a stark white hospital room with bars on the windows, white walls, and floors. I was in a crib and felt confined. I did not know anyone in the room, nor were nurses caring for me. The hospital had a policy that parents could only visit children once a day during the two-hour visiting time. I had just had major plastic surgery on my face with seventy-seven stitches. I had just gone through the most traumatic experience in my life. Even so, I was going through it alone in my mind. My dad had to go home to take care of the rest of my siblings, and my mom stayed with our Aunt Margaret and her family in Allentown while I was in the hospital.

In the hospital room with me were two other little girls. They were just as scared as I was, and I vividly remember every detail about them. One girl's name was Carol, and she was a petite blonde girl with blue eyes. She had her tonsils taken out. I remember her crying a lot, but looking back, I cried just as much. The other girl, named Anne, had short brown hair and was in the hospital for cystic fibrosis. She was the strongest of the three of us. She did not cry as much as the other two of us. She may have had more hospital experience and was numb to it.

Being in the hospital felt uncertain, and I did not know what was happening. I felt out of control and very alone. I do not have any positive memories of my time in the hospital.

I cannot picture any of the nurses in my head. I assume that it is because they were the ones who had to deliver pain and heartache to me. They would wake me up before breakfast and give me a shot in my butt. That was a horrible way to be woken up. The nurses consoled me while injecting the shot. Later I realized that they gave me antibiotics to keep me from getting an infection after the facial plastic surgery.

Every day in the hospital was traumatic. The smells, the chill, the stark whiteness of the environment, the bars on the windows, the cribs that contained us, and the needle stuck in my buttocks every morning are what my body and mind remember. I was all alone, and no fun activities could have distracted me from that horrible feeling. In 1970, they kept you in the hospital for longer than they do today. I spent a week in the hospital and remember nothing good from the experience.

Mom and my oldest sister Paula were only allowed to visit me during hospital visiting hours. Can you imagine the trauma of having to leave your four-year-old child in a hospital by herself as she cried and screamed in horror? The nurses distracted us by rides in a little red wagon so our families could sneak out. Every visit created new trauma, as each time my family left, I felt abandoned all over again. That little red wagon soon became a trauma trigger for me as I learned that it meant my family would be taken away from me again. As an adult, my sister Paula told me that she and Mom would go to the lobby and cry after they left me. I never knew that at the time. It makes me tear up as I type these words. Later, my mom told me that a Carpenter's song, "Close to You," reminded her of me and kept her strong during my hospital say. It became our song.

When I got home, we did not talk about the accident. It was 1970, and the attitude was that unspoken issues would magically disappear. Also, in the 1970s was a stigma around mental health. Society and medical professionals did not acknowledge or realize that anyone other than men going to war could have symptoms of post-traumatic stress syndrome.

Even then, trauma was often denied and was seen as a weakness if you spoke about it. So, the unspoken norm was to "suck it up and get over it." Getting over it and not processing the trauma have proven to be ineffective methods for dealing with trauma, as illustrated by the Adverse Childhood Experiences (ACEs) research.

My entire family was traumatized by the car accident, but I never knew that until much later.

My dad ended up having PTSD and drank too much to self-medicate. He was a functional alcoholic and would have had a breakdown if he did not drink. Drinking alcohol was society's coping strategy of choice back then. It was an acceptable form of self-medication and still is in many ways.

All I knew was that I felt abandoned. I was neglected emotionally and did not realize it. Childhood emotional neglect (CEN) is described as the parent's failure to meet their child's emotional needs, such as attention and support during the early years. In the 1970s, childhood emotional neglect was unrecognized, common, and seen as normal, especially in large families. A child needs a parent who is emotionally attuned to their needs, and this is difficult in a large family as ours. Because it's an *act of omission*, it's not visible, noticeable, or memorable (Webb, 2012). The car accident compounded these effects for me. I developed self-doubt that became the greatest barrier to my healing.

Loving parents can emotionally neglect children, as they were likely emotionally neglected themselves. Adults often did anything possible to distract themselves from the pain. Sometimes even positive things were used to self-medicate, such as over-working. Too much of a good thing can be harmful. Now we know much more about the impact of denial of mental health issues and trauma. Now it is understood that *not* talking about it and sucking it up is more detrimental than previously thought. We did not know what we didn't know.

I forgive myself for buying into the lie I was not worthy of fighting for after the accident and that my emotional needs were not important. The truth is that I was/am worthy, and my family followed the hospital policies and was respectful. My emotional needs were neglected by loving parents who struggled with their own feelings of overwhelm, discouragement, anxiety, and guilt from not being able to take care of my needs.

Chapter 2

No Safety in a Post-Accident World—What Is Wrong with Me?

As it turned out, I had full-blown PTSD with panic attacks for most of my childhood after the accident. I remember every instance and the surrounding smells, sounds, sights, and feelings when I was triggered by something from the car accident and subsequent hospitalization. The primary triggers were thunderstorms and riding in a car with someone whose driving made me uncomfortable.

I became a little meteorologist or a little storm tracker. I always knew when a storm was coming. I was hypervigilant of every cloud, thunderclap, lightning flash, scent of rain, and breeze that indicated a pending storm. I would do anything possible to avoid being in a situation where I could not quickly get to my mom, or other adults, who I felt would protect me and comfort me if I had a panic attack. I did not call them panic attacks at the time, but now I know what they were. My mom and oldest siblings—especially my oldest sisters—were my safe people.

Social anxiety showed up as I avoided doing any activity or being somewhere during the summer when there were chances of thunderstorms. I had subtle behaviors, but they were my flight response to get away from my feelings of anxiety and panic attacks. I needed to feel emotionally and physically safe, or I could not enjoy whatever activity I was experiencing at the time. I was embarrassed by this and thought that something was wrong with me. I struggled with this into my early teen years. Even when I arranged these situations, I still had panic attacks.

One summer, my oldest sister Paula took my sister Lisa and me to the beach at Ocean City, NJ, for a bit of vacation. Lisa is eight years older than me, and we had an excellent relationship growing up. We were both still young during this getaway.

We spent one day on the beach, and I remember it as a peaceful and fun day. The ocean water was a comfortable temperature with the smell of salt in the air. I played in the sand and waves feeling right a home. There was no threat of severe weather, and I did okay. The next day was rainy and cloudy, so we spent time on the boardwalk. Then, a thunderstorm started brewing over the ocean. The skies filled with ominous black clouds, and the wind was starting to whip up. We looked for a place to sit and wait out the storm and ended up at a pizza place on the boardwalk. The entire front wall of the shop was made of glass. The windows allowed me to see what was going on with the weather and the ocean. Even though watching the storm was scary, that was better than not knowing what was coming.

Seeing the storm helped me feel more comfortable and in control than if I were in a closed building where I did not know what was going on outside. Not knowing would have freaked me out. My sisters wanted to see the James Bond movie *Live and Let Die* in the theater to wait out the storm. When they mentioned this, I had a panic attack and started feeling light-headed and clammy just thinking about being inside a building. I felt like my life depended on knowing what was going on outside.

Another instance of anxiety happened when I was in third grade; I went to girl scout camp just for a day. My mom would typically be there because she was a girl scout leader. Most of the time, at girl scout events, I felt safe because my mom was with me. However, she was not at this camp because she worked at her paying job.

While at camp, a thunderstorm raged in, and I had a full-blown panic attack. I was sobbing uncontrollably and shaking as I hid behind a door inside a food-serving building. I do not remember who the woman was, but a girl scout leader found me and stayed with me, trying to calm me down. I could not calm down until the storm was over. After the storm faded away, I was so embarrassed.

All those things were burned into my memory because they were such extreme sensory experiences. I had no control over my environment. They're burned into my brain like the ten commandments were burned on the stone tablets in the Charlton Heston movie, never to be erased. Forty to fifty years have passed since these incidents, and I can still see every detail in my head.

I was an athletic child and always wanted to be better at whatever sport I was doing. Sports were those protective factors that I was good at and made me feel better. My self-esteem was still low, and sports provided a way to boost it, but I never felt remarkably successful.

I hid behind sports too. I tried to be tough, so people would not see the scared little girl. I was not strong at all, though. I had a lot of trouble sticking up for myself. I did not know how to advocate for myself and speak out when someone was bullying me or saying nasty things to me. Nor did I feel worthy enough to speak up for or set healthy boundaries for myself.

I was already getting tall in fourth grade, and the athletics I participated in made me strong and fit. I was only ten years old, but the older boys had already liked me. Several eighth-grade boys had a nickname for me that I did not understand at the time. They would call me "Skin." I hated it because of how they looked at me when they said it made me feel dirty. I had no idea why they called me that at the time, and I still do not fully understand it. Another younger boy called me "Legs." That was a challenging year for me. I felt alone and did not tell anyone about what they were saying to me. I thought I had done something to get those names; I didn't realize it was about my looks. I learned to shrink myself so people wouldn't see me. At that age, my voice was still weak, and this further took away any shred of self-respect that I had. So, I wore the blame for the name-calling rather than placing it on the boys who produced them. They were the ones with the issue, not me. So, I got my hair cut short into a pixie cut. It was like Samson getting his locks cut and taking away his strength.

My two oldest brothers were incredibly involved in sports. They both went to public high school, and the rest of us went to a Catholic high school in another town. My dad went to every one of their sporting events, both at home and when they traveled. My mom also went, and they took me with them. I loved those experiences. I got to know all their friends, and they called me Annie. Most people didn't call me that as I was not too fond of it, but I liked it when it came from someone close to me. It was a term of affection that made me feel good.

The only time I spent with my dad was either going to one of my brothers' sporting events or watching sports on TV. I could name the entire New York Yankees baseball team of the 1970s because my dad was a huge fan. The Miami Dolphins was his favorite football team because they had a Hungarian coach, Don Shula. My dad was immensely proud of his Hungarian heritage, and he expressed that regularly. He also liked the Pittsburgh Steelers, and we watched basketball too. I became obsessed with learning sporting facts as I thought it would be a way to connect with my dad.

I also had many positive things in my life at this time. I worshipped my older siblings, who often took me to do fun things they didn't have the opportunity to do as kids. Many protective factors balanced out the impact of the trauma. The protective factors didn't take away the trauma, but they gave me the strength to build skills that would serve me well for the rest of my life. I was a gifted athlete and picked up almost any sport I played.

I was on the girls' basketball team and a cheerleader for boys' basketball in the CYO league at our school. I was on the all-star team for both basketball and cheerleading every year I participated. My coach, Mrs. Rossi, made me the captain in eighth grade, and she trusted me to do what was best for the team. That boosted my self-esteem. She was a considerable influence on me and encouraged me to get better at basketball. My low self-esteem prevented me from becoming a ball hog. I was more of a defensive player and always backed up my teammates. That was an unintended positive aspect to my low self-esteem.

My mom was the swim team coach at one of the local high schools and a lifeguard and swim instructor at the Knoebels' Grove Amusement Park's Crystal Pool. I could go to work with my mom, so I was always near her during the summer. Being near her made it easier for me to avoid having severe panic attacks during thunderstorms. I also made many friends during that time with whom I'm still friends. I have fond memories of those times at Knoebels.

Sister Driving—Flight from Panic Attack

Another traumatic situation happened when I was eight years old. My sister, who is eight years older than me, was learning how to drive. She had her driver's permit, and my mom often let her drive the car home from Knoebels, which was about a fifteen-minute drive. My mom pulled onto the side of the road on a two-lane highway in my current hometown. I immediately got out of the car because I knew she would let Lisa drive. My poor sister didn't do anything to deserve my reaction. She just wanted to learn to drive. Even so, she experienced the consequences of my panic attack. I wasn't comfortable with many people driving. It was another instance of my fight-or-flight reaction.

Nothing anyone could ever do or say would conquer those fears. My family tried to calm me down when I had a panic attack, but it never worked. I understand kids who have extreme reactions to something that may seem like it is nothing to other people. Our brains respond to perceived threats without warning. The response is to fight or run from danger. We may feel out of control. It feels very dismissive when people say, "What were you thinking? Why can't you just stop it?" Our brains are wired to think or act for survival and, in times of fear, cannot reason.

I couldn't stop it, and I was only a kid. I couldn't control my brain, thoughts, actions, or words. Nothing was going to stop it until I felt safe. Kids with a history of trauma often express behaviors that look out of control. We often see them as bad kids making bad choices. That's always what I thought about myself. *What's wrong with me? Why can't I get over this? I'm not strong. I must be weak.* As I got older and realized what had happened to me and what I'd been through, I had the epiphany that it was not "what's wrong with me" but, more accurately, "what happened to me." It was not my fault that I wasn't "getting over it." I was just a kid, and no words, actions, or thoughts I could have done or should have done could stop the panic attacks. They weren't going to stop until I had healed. True healing never comes from ignorance of the problem.

> *I forgive myself for buying into the lie that something was wrong with me. The truth is that I went through traumas that impacted every aspect of my life. But understandably, I would have challenges after everything that happened. Our environment shapes us, and we cannot just ignore our struggles and use our will to overcome every challenge.*

Chapter 3

1980's-1993— Don't Let Anyone See the Real You; You'll Scare Them Away.

Around fourteen years old, my panic attacks seemed to stop. I thought *I'm just growing up and getting over it.* I was tired of feeling out of control and just wanted a "normal" life. I felt damaged because I felt so broken. I had major abandonment issues, but I didn't see the impact of those issues until much later.

I was starting a new phase in my life and going into high school. I was excited to see many friends I made at Knoebel's and from playing basketball as we all went to the same high school. I wanted to put my past behind me, including everything related to the car accident.

Before 1980, Post-traumatic stress disorder (PTSD) wasn't recognized as something that affected anyone outside the military. In 1980, PTSD first appeared as an operational diagnosis in the Diagnostic and Statistical Manual of the American Psychiatric Association (DSM-III). It was revised in DSM-III-R in 1987 and DSM-IV in 1994. It first appeared in the International Classification of Disease (ICD) system in

1992. For the first time, it was recognized that anyone who had experienced trauma could develop post-traumatic stress disorder.

With all this added information and awareness of trauma experienced by other populations, I started to recognize and acknowledge that I may have had PTSD. That was the extent of my realization, though. I wasn't ready to do anything about it. I just noticed it existed and that it may have impacted me.

When I entered high school, I also started drinking alcohol. In my small town, the joke was that there were bars and churches on every block. Drinking was a normal part of life, a badge of honor or a rite of passage. Because it was acceptable, drinking to self-medicate my mental health issues didn't raise any red flags. This lack of awareness and ability to talk about trauma perpetuated the symptoms and the maladaptive coping strategies I used for most of my life. I thought my symptoms of PTSD had stopped, but I realized that I had started drinking to self-medicate and subdue my pain. It was the first socially acceptable thing that effectively stopped my panic attacks.

I remember the first party I ever went to as a freshman in high school. I drank five Colt 45 beers in about a two-hour time frame. I got so drunk that I threw up at this friend's house. I was embarrassed. I didn't know I was trying to numb my pain; drinking was the only thing I had control over at the time. Ironically, it made me even more out of control. However, I can say that my panic attacks stopped right about the same time. Drinking at the age of fourteen and beyond did explicitly one thing for me. It stopped the feeling that I was damaged, and I didn't feel pain anymore—until I woke up the next day. Numbing myself using alcohol led to a depression that I didn't understand or acknowledge for many years.

I drank heavily throughout my high school years and into my early thirties. It was the only resource that helped control my panic attacks and anxiety. I didn't know anything else and didn't understand why I was drinking at the time.

It felt good to drink and made me feel like an adult. I was proud that I could do an entire beer bong in one shot. It was a badge of honor that people around me reinforced. That attitude around alcohol was and is part of society's acceptance of alcohol use. Yet underneath, it also created feelings of worthlessness and ambivalence that heavily impacted my self-worth. They were subtle feelings that did not raise any red flags for people around me. This drain on my self-worth was like a dripping faucet that no one noticed. Instead, I internalized the shame that welled within me from excessive drinking. I had superficial self-worth that relied on my good looks, athletic ability, and popularity, which eventually was shattered by failure.

I had a significant romantic relationship in my junior year of high school at sixteen. That's when I lost my virginity. I thought this relationship would be for the rest of my life. It was solid, or so I thought, for the first year. He broke up with me, the first significant failure rocking my world. I couldn't eat or sleep, and I lost weight. I went down to 111 pounds; at 5 feet 7 inches tall, that was a big hit. Ironically, my friends praised me for how I looked. Teachers, on the other hand, noticed me falling apart. I remember my typing teacher putting her hand on my shoulder as I left class. She shuddered because she could feel my shoulder bones. She said, "Annie, I'm worried about you." I told her I was okay and knew I needed to gain weight, but deep down, I felt good wearing size zero clothes. I brushed off her concern like it was nothing, but that was the first time someone showed concern for me other than my mom. I lived on autopilot for so long that I felt uncomfortable with someone noticing my pain. I felt like she looked into my soul that day and saw the real me for the first time. She taught me that I could not underestimate how one caring adult can have a powerful and positive impact on a child or youth.

Looking back, I was using the romantic relationship to fill in the holes in my self-esteem. Filling holes with relationships is what you do in high school. I was living in the moment and didn't know what I didn't know. I wasn't in a place to have a healthy relationship with anyone because I didn't have a healthy relationship with myself. I didn't know how to love myself. That was the first significant failure *and* breakthrough in my life. I survived and learned many things about myself and others, but I didn't see it at the time.

I was very needy in relationships. I felt I wasn't worthy or good enough because I was somehow damaged. I was desperate to have a boyfriend and to have someone love me for me and not my fantasy of me. No one saw the "real" me—but in fairness, I always hid the real me and kept trying to prove myself throughout my childhood into adulthood. This translated to perfectionism. I put on a brave face and wore a mask, hiding the real me from others. I strived for things to look good on the outside and didn't care about this choice affecting my emotions and self-worth. My attachment style to people was disorganized because of the inconsistency of relationships in my childhood. Being a perfectionist was easy because it gave me a consistent form to which I could attach my identity. Perfectionism is a double edge sword. I was successful in many ways, but it has eaten away at my well-being over the years. It turns out perfectionism has been one of the most challenging things to overcome.

Just because something looks good on the outside doesn't mean it *is* good. If you saw my life during my teenage and young adult years, you would have no clue what was happening under the surface. I was popular, pretty, and incredibly involved in student government. I dated the football team captain and was the prom's princess. I even won the "girl who lives her faith the most" award as I was hungover at my Catholic high school graduation. It was a joke to me when I heard it. These so-called "accomplishments" were the shaky foundation of my perfectionist life. Nothing would fill the holes in my self-worth until I did it for myself.

In 1987, I moved to California to attend school and grow up. I always felt like my siblings didn't have any respect for me because my life was "easier" compared to theirs. I felt I wasn't worth anything and wanted to prove myself to everyone. The reality is that my parents didn't have enough money to pay for all their children to attend college. We all had to make our own way, and our parents supported us however they could.

I moved to the San Francisco Bay Area and, for six months, stayed with my brother and his new bride. During that time, I found a job and set up a residency in California to go to school for free or almost free. I wanted to be a physical therapist, so college was necessary. Attaining my degree was part of striving to prove myself. I spent so much of my childhood battling PTSD and trying to prove I was worthy, but the harder I tried, the less I succeeded.

In January 1988, I started school at San Francisco State University. I attended school full-time, worked three jobs, and trained to be an athletic trainer. I took out several student loans because the cost of living was high and working three jobs wasn't cutting it. So, at the age of twenty-one, I appeared to be a hard-working student commuter making it all work while being across the country from the rest of her family.

I earned my bachelor's degree from San Francisco State and became an Athletic Trainer Certified (ATC). I had some exciting jobs on a few research studies at Stanford University and worked at a physical therapy clinic. We worked with the San Francisco 49ers team doctors' group. I thought I was cool.

I forgive myself for buying into the lie that I needed to be "perfect" and not show anyone the pain on the inside. The truth is that my family and friends loved me no matter the façade I wore. Being vulnerable is not a weakness but a strength. Sharing my story has made me stronger. I have influenced others and made it safe for them to share their stories.

The Ultimate Violation

I was a small-town girl in a big city, and I loved it, but I was also very naive and ripe for being used and abused. I was so insecure. My looks and athleticism attracted men often, though the relationships were superficial. My insecurity screamed to these men, who took advantage or ran the other way. I was highly needy in relationships and just wanted someone to love me.

When I was at a party at school, I met a guy I will call Trey, who was attractive. He paid a lot of attention to me, and I got caught up in his charm. That was the beginning of a complicated relationship that would change my life in ways I couldn't have imagined. We had intimate relations, but it wasn't much more than that. We didn't go on dates but hooked up instead. We met once every other week, as it started to feel uncomfortable for me. So, I began to keep my distance because I felt worse about myself after being with him.

One Saturday night, I went to a party in San Francisco with some new college friends. I didn't know the people having the party, but my friends did. It was one of the first parties I attended at school, as I was still getting to know people. I hadn't seen Trey for about three weeks until I saw him at this party near campus. Trey approached me and asked me to go to his car to talk. I didn't want to go, but I always tried to please others. I didn't want to disappoint him. I thought that he just wanted to talk more privately. I was so naïve. When we got to the car, he asked me to get in the back seat. Once I was in the back seat, he got on top of me. I told him I didn't want to have sex, but he kept telling me that we had already been intimate, and this would be quick. I said no a few more times, but I thought it would be rude to fight him since I went out there with him and "led him on." His cousin stood outside of the car and watched. After it was over, I returned to the party but didn't stay much longer. I didn't say anything to my friends about what had happened.

I didn't even realize it was rape at the time because I knew and dated him. Date rape wasn't something people talked about at the time. So, I blamed myself for it happening and tried to shake it off. It took months before I realized I was raped. Later that same year, I was at another party near campus, and several football players were there. I had just arrived when one of the football players pulled me into a room and started kissing me. Things shifted fast, and he raped me. I blamed myself again.

About a year and a half later, I was sleeping at my studio apartment on a Saturday night when the security buzzer rang. It was 2 a.m., and I groggily woke up to answer the buzzer. It was Trey wanting to "talk." I was the naive girl who believed he just wanted to talk. When he came to the apartment, he had a cousin with him I didn't know. When I saw the two of them, I tried to keep the door closed, but they pushed it open. I kept telling him I wanted them to leave, but he would not listen. So, he followed me around the apartment. I tried to go into the bathroom, and he opened the door. I couldn't go anywhere to escape him. I lived above a bar, so no one would hear me even if I screamed.

He raped me while his cousin watched. He tried to get his cousin to join in, but the cousin refused. He saw how I was fighting and didn't want to be involved. They finally left, and I just went back to sleep. I wanted to forget the whole thing and "get over it," as I did from the earlier trauma in my life. Or so I thought. The following Monday night, I was out with a few friends. We went to a bar for happy hour. Then, as we were in the club dancing, I started having a panic attack. I needed to walk outside because I felt so out of control. Every part of my being just wanted to get out of that bar and get away from other people.

Even though I was outside, I felt claustrophobic at that moment, which had never happened to me. One of my friends came out and asked me what was wrong. Then, suddenly, I realized that I had been raped by Trey two nights earlier. I told my friend what happened, and she told me to get professional help and talk to the police. She was incredibly supportive, which made a difference in speaking out. After the previous rapes, I didn't tell anyone what happened until much later. I was too embarrassed and thought I had done something to ask for it.

The following day, I went to the police and filed a report. I didn't press charges. I couldn't even imagine having to go through a trial and tell my story. It was too painful, and I was embarrassed and terrified. My family was on the East Coast, and I expected they wouldn't want to talk about it. So, I didn't feel I'd have support if I chose to press charges.

The police called me after filing the report and asked if I wanted to reconsider and press charges. They informed me that the guy who had raped me had also come up in other police reports as raping women. I still couldn't bring myself to press charges. I felt too alone to take that on.

I went to counseling shortly after the third rape. I told the counselor, "I had PTSD as a kid, but I got over it." Those were my exact words. I only went to two or three counseling sessions; proper healing was still far off. As I author this book and share my experiences of rape, I still feel some shame, but it has much less power over me. The search for my self-worth would continue to the next phase of life. After experiencing all these traumas, I decided to move across the country again and return to the East Coast.

> *I forgive myself for buying into the lie that I deserved to be raped or asked for it by not fighting enough. The truth is that the shame and my low self-esteem put me at risk of being sexually assaulted. It was not my fault. I did not know how to advocate for myself, let alone know that I could fight for myself. The perpetrators preyed on me because they saw my shame and used it to take advantage of me.*

Chapter 4

You Can Run, but You Can't Hide from Pain

After everything I experienced in California, I was ready for a fresh start in my life. In hindsight, I was running away from the pain and further trauma I experienced in San Francisco. I thought moving this time would be different because I had a college degree, and the cost of living was lower in Florida. I believed in the fantasy that if I moved to a new place, my life would start fresh, as if nothing had ever happened. My heart knew this couldn't be accurate, but my brain was still in survival mode and wanted it to be the reality.

The impacts of the lifelong trauma looked different at that point in my life. I was self-medicating with alcohol, partying with friends, searching for a relationship with all the wrong guys, and throwing myself into my career. I left California with a vision of a clean slate. But I was living the same patterns. I numbed the pain and used various other escapes to become someone different, someone, who wasn't damaged goods. I had a false belief that I was indestructible when the reality was that I was still the scared little girl in the hospital.

Leaving California was bittersweet. I was leaving my friends, but it wasn't enough to keep me from running away.

I left in March of 1993 and drove the southern US route back to the East Coast, so I didn't have to drive in the snow. On my way home, I stopped in Tampa to visit my best friend, Judy, who used to live in California. She moved to Florida a few years earlier, and we stayed connected. It felt good to be with someone familiar while leaving my friends behind in the Bay Area.

I visited Judy for about a week, and we had a fabulous time. Nothing had changed between us, and we partied like it was 1999, just a little early. We went to the beach, hung out by the pool at her apartment complex, and partied at clubs in the Tampa Bay area. It was spring break season, so it was extra busy, and the area was full of people partying from all over the country. I didn't know anyone other than Judy, which made it all easier. No one knew my past or anything about me.

That was my MO, wanting to start fresh so that no one saw who I was inside or the pain I had endured. They saw the superficial me—fun, athletic, and attractive, with blonde hair and a great tan. I liked it that way, and that mask of attractiveness made it easier to hide who I really was. Unfortunately, others noticed my false front and didn't show me their true selves either. Looking back, it was like a play with everyone acting in their roles to continue to feed the hiding of my true self from others and myself.

While visiting Judy, we went to a club in Ybor City, the French Quarters of Tampa. It was a fantastic club with great music. I had been in Tampa for a few days and worked on my tan. I was in the best shape of my life from the running and swimming I had been doing in California. I was standing next to Judy, drinking a beer, and checking out the scene. I must have looked like fresh meat to the guys at the club because they had never seen me before.

Judy danced with a guy, and another guy started making his way toward me as I was alone. Even though I put off a confident vibe, fear lurked inside me. I drank another beer to keep it at bay. This guy, Frank, finally came to talk to me. We talked for a while, and he seemed nice. I didn't feel like he was trying to get in my pants. We had a lot in common, as he was an athlete and was getting into the professional world of track and field. He was a sprinter who ran the 400-meter hurdles and was looking for a trainer.

Frank and I talked that night, and he kept it very cordial. I was excited by the prospect of meeting a professional athlete and got sucked into that world again. It felt safe because he only wanted to be friends. Then, two days later, Judy and I returned to the same club, and Frank was there. We exchanged phone numbers, and he asked me to move to Florida to be his personal athletic trainer. It sounded like a fantastic opportunity, and Judy was excited I'd live in the same area as her again.

After I visited with Judy, I drove the rest of the way home to Pennsylvania over the next few days. I visited other friends along the way. Socializing was another way I self-medicated. The excitement of going to novel places and meeting new people was like a drug for me. It kept me from dealing with the wounds deep inside that continued to tear through me like piranhas.

My original plan after leaving California was to settle near my oldest sister in New Jersey. We were always close, and her husband was like a dad or big brother to me. He always watched out for me and was one of the few people who wanted to hurt the guy who raped me. So, I moved in with them and stayed there for ten months until I figured out the next steps in my career.

I finally moved to Tampa in 1994. When I got there, the job fell through with the sprinter. It was another disappointment as I started my new life in Florida. So, I got a waitressing job and later a position as an athletic trainer at a physical therapy clinic.

Moving to Florida didn't make my life's pain and trauma disappear. I continued to search for and try to prove my self-worth. I was committed to making that happen, no matter what.

I started dating Eli while working at the physical therapy clinic. The relationship felt deeper than the ones I had in California. We moved in together, and I thought I had finally made it. I was now worthy of having a better relationship. But it turns out, again, it was only on the surface. I still hid the pain and continued to drink, even though I didn't binge drink as much as I had previously. I redirected my focus to training for triathlons and attempted to learn how to surf. I even quit my job to start a travel business with Eli. I was still trying to prove my worth.

I was wounded in many ways and didn't want to face it. Eventually, Eli and I broke up, and I found myself without a job and no place to live. I stayed with several friends who helped me, but my self-worth took a bigger hit than any previous experiences. I gave up who I was during my relationship with Eli, but I thought that's what one does when in love. Now I was left with nothing after I gave up everything else for him.

My friends were amazing and supported me through this challenging time. I moved in with a friend, and another friend got me a job working with two children with developmental disabilities. I thought it would be temporary, but it ended up being the beginning of a life-changing career working with children and adults with disabilities.

> *I forgive myself for believing that if people knew the real me, they wouldn't love me. The truth is that my vulnerability would connect me to people if I allowed it. The wall I put up prevented them from really loving me because they did not know me. I am lovable, and I am enough with the scars and strengths together.*

Chapter 5

Chaos to Zen—Breakthrough

In 1998, after several failed relationships and moving to the Tampa Bay area, I knew something needed to change. I couldn't run from myself anymore and leaned into my new job. I loved working with children with behavior problems and felt I understood them. I also realized that I was good at it. I have sincere empathy for people who struggle in life. I finally became the person I was meant to be through this work with children and adults with disabilities.

The family that I worked with became like my family away from home. They trusted me with their children and encouraged me to start my own home health business working with children and adults with disabilities. This life seemed familiar to me, and I felt like I was finally living into my worth from the inside rather than constantly trying to prove my worth to others.

I excitedly started my business. I tend to be impulsive—more on my ADHD adventures later—when making decisions, which doesn't always work out for me. Thank God my memory is short and doesn't stop me from jumping into scary things. I felt empowered to develop the framework and all the policies and protocols for my business. That sounds strange, but it felt very freeing, and I didn't have to run it by anyone until it was finished. I felt like I was indeed in control of my career for the first time in my life. It was *my* business, and I was going to make it work!

I started out doing all the work myself for the first year. I provided respite and residential habilitation services for families, companion services, homemaker services, and supported living for adults with disabilities living independently. My business reputation snowballed in the first year. By the end of that year, I began hiring people to deliver services. I grew my business by 300 percent by the end of the first year. It was satisfying, and I felt so accomplished. I also met a Board-Certified Behavior Analyst through work. I didn't know what this work was, but it immediately intrigued me. Again, it felt familiar, and I was naturally good at supporting children with behavior problems. I got them, as I was one of those kids, but I internalized my behaviors. I wanted to give children the support that I never had.

My business was thriving, I had a lovely two-bedroom apartment in South Tampa, and I was content with how my life was going. I had many friends and felt like I had succeeded in things I hadn't done before, or so I thought. Yet I still felt a hole inside me, but I couldn't identify it. My love life was still lacking, and I felt needy and desperate with men. I looked at *any* guy that showed interest in me as a potential boyfriend. I scared many guys away. I didn't know what I needed to do to get rid of this neediness. Unbeknownst to me, depression made me numb to feelings for anyone. I even kept my friends at arm's length so they wouldn't see the real me. My outer shell of perfection began to crack even though I self-medicated with my looks, fitness, work, and superficial relationships.

Though my low self-worth started with the childhood trauma, it hit a new low in my early thirties because I was still single and had no children. My family wasn't pressuring me to get married and have children. I felt pressure from watching many friends I grew up with in Pennsylvania who were now married and having children. They were living my version of an ideal life, and I felt like I was a failure because I didn't have that life. I lost touch with many of those friends because I felt terrible about myself when talking to them. I know they felt like I abandoned them, but you can't give yourself what you don't have.

My relationship with my dad was distant during this period. During the spring of 1998, I visited my family, and he said something to me that would further lower my self-esteem. We were at my brother Joe's house watching the women's basketball finals with Joe's wife and my mom and dad. I told my dad, "I'm surprised you are watching women's basketball because you never came to see me play."

His response has been blazed in my head ever since. He said, "Why would I go to see you play basketball? It was boring."

I was shocked. Mom scolded him in a non-scolding way. I appreciated her support, but his words hung in the room like the smoke from a smelly cigar that wouldn't go away. I didn't know what to say. I just sat there with my eyes like saucers and shook my head. The truth finally came out, and it hurt a lot.

> *I forgive myself for buying into the lie that my life had to be full and complete, with a husband, family, and career by the time I turned thirty. The truth is that I do not need to have life all figured out, and I can follow my dreams. I do not have to live up to someone else's standard of a complete and fulfilling life. I am enough and worthy every day in every situation. This is true freedom!*

Awakening of the Soul

Back in Tampa, I started going to a Catholic church near my apartment. The Catholic church in Florida was vastly different than churches in Pennsylvania. It was more progressive and had more contemporary music. It reminded me of when I was in high school. It filled me up and made me want to go more often.

I hadn't attended church regularly since my first year in California back in 1987. My life was not reflecting Jesus, and I was ashamed. Attending church was a tool I hadn't tried to help lift myself out of my funk. I'll never forget the priest there, Father Mike. He was young, and his messages were practical to my life. I felt welcomed there.

Father Mike had a glass of milk on the pulpit one Sunday. He put chocolate syrup in the milk as he talked. He used it as an analogy for our lives. Sometimes we feel like milk with chocolate syrup sitting at the bottom of the glass. He mixed the milk with a spoon to stir up the syrup. He said, "Sometimes we need to stir things up in our lives to feel whole again." A CHOICE singles Christian weekend retreat was coming up, and he suggested I attend. It piqued my interest, so I signed up. I was excited about it and knew it was the right time to move into the next level of my life.

I was thirty-three when I went to the singles Christian retreat. It was held at the Curcillo Center in the Ybor City section of Tampa, Florida. Many people my age were at the retreat, and I felt right at home. It was a weekend of pampering with excellent meals and a time to focus on my relationship with God.

The retreat was set up by a team of singles, a married couple, and a priest. Each person shared a story about their own experiences during their CHOICE retreat weekend and how it changed their lives or how they overcame something difficult in their lives with God's help as a result. It targeted all Christians, but there was a strong Catholic influence. The music inspired me and opened my heart to healing. I remember Michael W. Smith's music being a big part of each session.

During that weekend, I had a major spiritual awakening. One of the activities revolved around forgiveness. Our task was to write a letter to someone in our lives we needed to forgive or ask for forgiveness from them. I wrote a letter to God to ask for forgiveness for all the sins I had committed in my life, especially as a young adult. I didn't feel worthy of God's love, but He touched my heart so profoundly that He broke the chains of trauma and pain in me. I cried uncontrollably while writing the letter. I was freed from all the misconceptions I had about myself. Writing the letter was cathartic, and I felt like chains were being broken.

I made some fantastic friends that weekend. I finally found my tribe and felt like a new person. God was working on me and giving me experiences of feeling loved like I never had. I was worthy of accepting God's plan for me so I could stop beating myself up, even for things out of my control.

By the end of the weekend, I decided to make some changes in my life, and one of them was to see if I could stop drinking— but not right away. I also decided to become celibate again. That was an easy decision because my intimate relationships had only brought me pain and left me feeling emptier. What I was using to fill myself was draining me of self-respect and love for myself. I wanted my life to be different and was ready for it.

The CHOICE community was vital for the weekend and afterward. I became a co-social chair with my new friend Anne—we became "The Annes"—and I dove headfirst into this new life. Some of my old friends were uncomfortable with my new choices in life, and I chose to leave those relationships because they held me to my old life. I needed to take care of myself first, and I finally felt confident to do that.

I finally found something that I was missing in my life previously. I now had a strong relationship with Jesus and felt whole. It was the beginning of a new phase in my life, and I was excited about it.

Another thing that came out of the CHOICE weekend was that I felt worthy of being near my family again. I was ashamed before and couldn't face them, even if they didn't say or do anything to make me feel that way. It was a lie I believed, and now it no longer had power over me.

> *I forgive myself for buying into the lie that my voice does not matter and that I cannot trust my gut. The truth is that my gut is the small little voice of God guiding me along. I need to listen to that voice and be silent more rather than constantly trying to prove myself and letting others dictate my life. When I live my purpose, I thrive, even if the path has challenges along the way.*

You are Worthy—Going Home

I decided to move back to Pennsylvania after my dad had a medical emergency and my godmother had cancer and passed away. I felt like God gave me a clear message that he wanted me to move back home. I didn't know what He had planned for me, but it's a message that has stayed in my head. I knew it was the right thing to do. I moved back to Pennsylvania in June 1999.

The downside of my choice to move back home was that I was leaving all my friends in Tampa. I met so many incredible people with who I felt a strong connection. I also knew they would *always* be my friends, and our connections would never break, even if I lived thousands of miles away. So, I moved one year to the day after my CHOICE weekend. My friends had a big going away party for me, making me feel even more loved than I could imagine.

I also had to sell my business. I met a physical therapist through CHOICE, and she was interested in buying it. She purchased the business, giving me enough money for a down payment on a house and some monthly funds to pay for living expenses while I was starting again in Pennsylvania.

In June 1999, I trekked back to Pennsylvania from Florida with a U-Haul truck while towing my car. I bought a townhouse in Coplay, right across the river from my brother Joe and his wife, Mary. Joe and I had always been close, and the Lehigh Valley was close enough to the rest of my family; it was an easy choice. The Lehigh Valley was also where the car accident that changed my life occurred. In the back of my mind, I was ready to face what had happened.

Toward the end of my time in Florida, I took a meditation course. I learned how to meditate and connect with God in everything I do. It took my faith and my relationship with God to the next level. My self-esteem grew further and gave me a new purpose in life. I continued to meditate after moving back to Pennsylvania, which gave me the strength to stop drinking alcohol entirely. At first, I wanted to see if I could do it. Once I stopped, I didn't give it a second thought. I also became vegetarian and lost the baggage I had been carrying. I went to retreats regularly at a Meditation Retreat Center in the Catskills.

Once I moved into my new townhouse, I applied to Lehigh University for the School Psychology program and wanted to become a Board-Certified Behavior Analyst (BCBA). I called the university to explore options for work-study jobs to help with tuition. I spoke to someone in the Special Education Department who told me about an open adult group home supervisor position. It paid all my tuition, and I would receive a stipend for living expenses. However, I needed to be enrolled in the Special Education program to take the position. They told me I could transfer to the School Psychology program later. I didn't end up transferring.

I ended up falling in love with the Special Education program and with the group home residents. We had a wonderful team of people working at the group home with me, and we all became a family. I *loved* the residents, and it was a rich and fulfilling experience. My education and work experiences gave me a new direction for what God had planned for me. I had no idea it would lead to the opportunities it did in my new life.

> *I forgive myself for buying into the lie that I needed to live away from home and my family to be successful and living in Pennsylvania meant failure to me. The truth is that I can be content with myself, no matter the situation or location. Living near family does not make me less or weak. They are a source of strength for me. Running from them is running from myself.*

Chapter 6

The Hard Work Begins...

The First Red Flag—Emotional Attack Relived

Being back home in Pennsylvania was fabulous, and it was easy to see any of my family. I was able to attend holiday events quickly. The first Thanksgiving I experienced while living back in Pennsylvania was an exciting event for me. I was *home*! As I was driving to the Thanksgiving dinner at my brother Tom's house, I started to have a panic attack. I didn't know what was happening as it had been such a long time since I had an attack. None of my previous triggers related to the car accident would make me connect the panic attack to that. So, I called a friend of mine and explained what was going on. They told me to talk to a professional counselor. I went to the Thanksgiving dinner and didn't mention anything to my family. So, I needed to figure out more about the panic attack first.

As I drove home from the family gathering, I felt a strong message from God that was clear as day. He said, "You've tried to heal on your own. Now it's time to heal with *my* help and professional help." I can hear His voice in my head so clearly, even after twenty-three years since this incident. It has guided my healing and now my professional work. It also gave me the strength to do the challenging work of digging into the pain and trauma from my life to this point, especially in the early part of my life.

The week following Thanksgiving, I made an appointment with my primary care doctor. He asked me to complete a survey and then diagnosed me with generalized anxiety disorder. I felt some peace with this as I could finally name what I had experienced my whole life. A name for the symptoms was only one piece of the puzzle. He referred me to get counseling, and it was the first time in my life that I was serious about treatment to heal the emotional pain I had gone through.

At the age of thirty-three, I finally went to counseling for an extended period. I felt ready to do the challenging work and dig into my pain. I do not doubt that if I didn't have my faith and relationship with God, this couldn't have been possible. I felt like I was feeling safe, seen, and heard on a deeper level. My therapist also validated what I had been through as being traumatic. There were still many things that I didn't realize then, but it was starting to chip away at the iceberg of childhood adversity and the adult trauma events that shrouded most of my life up to that point.

Early counseling involved exploring my symptoms, some of which were under control with the medication. I shared my childhood trauma for the first time with someone in more depth than ever before. It felt good to receive validation that my childhood trauma experiences were significant and the primary cause of my struggles.

In early 2000 I started treatment, and I didn't yet know about the Adverse Childhood Experiences Study (ACES). I knew intuitively that the trauma influenced me in many ways, yet I didn't have an awareness of the natural impacts until years later. The more I study ACES, the more I connect the dots to my experiences. This growing awareness has been freeing, and over time my family became more willing to discuss the car accident to shed some light on things. Unfortunately, I didn't realize how much the accident affected them at the time. It is easy to want to move on from painful traumas, but they will come back to haunt you in some way if you don't dig into your trauma with professional help. Professional help for childhood trauma has been up for debate and has evolved since the ACES study.

After attending about a year of counseling, I thought I was "fixed." At least fixed enough to live a more peaceful life and feel more confident in myself. My faith and relationship with God continued to grow through all of this. I meditated daily, refrained from drinking alcohol, and continued a vegetarian diet. I embraced healing physically, mentally, and emotionally.

I trained heavily by running, biking, and swimming to compete in triathlons and running races. I loved this physical activity and had access to a nine-mile trail looping around the town of Coplay. It was easy to keep up with regular exercise, and I became leaner and had more vitality.

The Second Red Flag—Physical Attack Relived

When I was getting my master's at Lehigh University, my job entailed being the supervisor of a group home for adults with special needs living in the community. I loved working with them, and they became my family. Even during chaotic behavioral incidents, I remember the laughs more than anything. My passion for working with children and adults with special needs constantly feeds me. No matter how hard the work became at times, the joy overshadowed the difficulties.

After a long weekend of work at the group home, my left elbow locked up and wouldn't straighten out. It was bent about fifteen degrees, and it was painful. I thought I injured it at work. I went to my primary care doctor, and he sent me to physical therapy. I went to PT for about two months, and the elbow improved. I still didn't know the trigger for it, but it improved enough for me to stop PT. It didn't stop me from doing all the other physical exercises I had already been doing.

About three months later, pain struck both knees unexpectedly. They didn't lock as the elbow did, but the pain was achy in the same way. I didn't do anything that would trigger this pain in my knees. So, I went to my doctor again, and he conducted a few tests. One of them was an anti-nuclear antibody (ANA) test. It came back positive, and he referred me to see a rheumatologist.

The rheumatologist conducted further testing, and I was diagnosed with systemic lupus erythematosus (SLE) and Sjogren's syndrome. These are two autoimmune diseases where the body attacks itself. All the symptoms and illnesses I had while living in California started to make sense now. My eyes were constantly dehydrated, a prominent symptom of Sjogren's syndrome. It was scary at first yet freeing to have a label for all the mystery symptoms I had been having. My rheumatologist put me on Plaquenil (hydroxychloroquine), an anti-malarial medication used to treat lupus and other autoimmune diseases. My eyes would need to be checked yearly to ensure the drug wasn't building up and damaging my eyes, a known side effect.

I was determined to do everything I could to manage my health naturally. God had previously gotten me through everything in my life, and it prepared me to take on this next challenge. I was confident that I could do it. So, I went to the Thomas Jefferson Center for Integrative Medicine at the suggestion of a friend. One of the first things my doctor suggested was to have my amalgam fillings removed and replaced to eliminate the mercury in my body. That would take a little more time to have done, but I began the journey of research on mercury side effects.

Dr. Foster at the TJ Center for Integrative Medicine ran further tests. He suggested I begin a gluten- and dairy-free diet and special supplements to address my deficiencies or improve my symptoms. I was already on a vegetarian diet and decided not to do the gluten-free and dairy-free diet. With everything else I was doing; it wasn't something that I thought I could do well. My intuition didn't buy into the dietary changes, so I'd find it difficult to maintain. I saw other specialists for my eyes and had plugs put into my tear ducts to keep moisture from draining out of my eyes. That procedure helped artificial drops to stay in my eye sockets and augment the moisture that was missing because of Sjogren's syndrome.

I wanted to continue my life as normally as possible and not let the health challenges I was dealing with stop me. I was in the best physical shape of my life, and this was just a speed bump in my life, or so I thought. I was diagnosed with only two autoimmune diseases; I figured it could be worse.

> *I forgive myself for buying into the lie that my life will be easy once I got over my childhood and young adult trauma. The truth is that I may go through challenges, and I know that God has my back and will carry me through if I let him. When I try to do everything on my own, I may succeed, but it will feel more difficult because I'm alone in my battle. God can use any trauma I have experienced to build and strengthen me. He doesn't create the trauma, but He will always be there for me if I let Him.*

Joy in the Little Things

Weekend with the Nieces

I enjoyed living back in Pennsylvania, especially hanging out with all my nieces and nephews. I was the "Cool Aunt" as I was much younger than all my siblings, so I was young enough to have a great friendship with the kids. I wanted to make up for all the time I lived away.

I had an "Aunt Weekend" with three of my nieces between the ages of eight to twelve. It was in the fall, and we spent the first day doing a corn maze and hayride on a local farm. The autumn colors in Pennsylvania are mesmerizing, and it was a perfect way to hang out with my nieces. We had dinner and watched a chick flick, *Where the Heart Is,* with Natalie Portman. We ate snacks, cuddled on the couch, and laughed at our niece Maura's extensive hair accessory collection. She now has a daughter of her own, and I know that her hair accessories will be put to beneficial use. It was great to have this time with them, and we laughed a lot. I smile as I think about the fun we had that weekend.

We went to Dorney Park Amusement Resort on the second day of the weekend. We had a joyful time on the roller coasters and with all the Halloween-themed activities throughout the park. I wanted to spend as many precious moments with my nieces and nephews as I could now that I lived back home.

Those simple things in life are the ones I cherish the most. The striving, as I once did in the past, only distracts me from these joys.

Weekend with the Nephews

A few months later, I had an "Aunt Weekend" with my nephews Eric and Jay. We went snowboarding at Camelback Ski Resort in the Poconos. My family joked that someone was going to be injured while I was watching them.

When I was about twelve years old, I was at my sister Trish's house and I was hanging out in their back yard with my two nieces. Melanie was four years old, and Margo was one. They were like my little sisters because we were so close in age. We were playing on their swing set on a gorgeous summer day. Trish was inside, so I was watching the girls. A few years older than my oldest niece, one of their neighbors played in the yard with us. We were hanging from the top of the swing set and jumping to the ground. Margo was in the yard watching and playing with other things. I received a phone call and went into the house to take it. While inside, Melanie jumped from the top bar and landed with her arm outstretched. The next moment, my sister was running down the yard holding Melanie, crying hysterically. Melanie broke her arm at the elbow when she landed and needed a trip to the emergency room. She required surgery to have pins put into her elbow to repair the break. Forty years later, she still tells the story of how I "broke her arm." It's a running joke, but I felt terrible that it happened.

I spent so much of my childhood doing things independently with little adult supervision, so I don't think, at the age of twelve, I knew the dangers of leaving a four-year-old child alone on a swing set. It's not an excuse. Melanie was traumatized. I wish I knew then what I know now.

I was determined to have an uneventful and injury-free time with my nephews. I helped them put on wrist guards, so neither would break their wrist if they fell while snowboarding. Unfortunately, I couldn't get them on myself. I laughed but went without wrist guards and didn't mention it to them. We had a fun time snowboarding and playing until the resort was about to close for the evening.

Toward the end of the evening, I took a spill, landing on my butt with an outstretched hand. As soon as my hand hit the ground, I felt something pop. My background as an athletic trainer alerted me immediately to my injury. It wasn't too painful, so I worked hard and finally put the wrist guards on myself. I didn't want to stop the boys from snowboarding, and I didn't want to stop either.

I think I don't ask for help because I don't want to put anyone else out, and it may come from that deep-seated feeling that I am not worthy of putting myself first. This unworthy feeling is one of those leftover emotions and beliefs from the trauma of the car accident and hospital stay when I was four years old. It imprinted in my mind that "no one will take care of me" and that I need to "suck it up and take care of myself" —or *not* take care of myself.

Somehow, I snowboarded for another hour with an injured wrist; I didn't let it stop me. I had fun boarding with my nephews. As we were packing up and getting ready to leave the resort, I told Eric and Jay that I thought I might have broken my wrist. They asked, "Why didn't you say something to us?" I told them I didn't want to stop having fun or interrupt their fun. This is a signal of the lingering self-doubt and lack of self-worth that remained.

The next day, Jay sat in the front seat and helped me shift the gears on my Nissan Maxima. My right wrist hurt, and I knew I needed to go to the ER. I dropped them off with their parents, headed to the ER for x-rays, and eventually got a cast. It was just another event in my life that I didn't think about very much. It was par for the course that I was somehow injured, and I would figure out a way to do everything I needed without asking for help. Even in my thirties, I still thought I wasn't good enough to ask for help. It wasn't something that even came to mind. I just adapted. That skill was a good thing in some ways, but emotionally distancing from others was still an issue for me. I didn't trust that someone could help me. That emotional scar would take the longest to get over. Bones heal quickly, but the impact of trauma becomes hard-wired in your brain. It's not something that heals overnight.

The Third Red Flag—Second Physical Attack Relived

I had more intensive symptoms during my first several years of being diagnosed with lupus and Sjogren's syndrome. Headaches came more frequently, and I had an EEG and CT scan of my head to identify issues. My brain scan showed a small spot on my brain, but it wasn't significant enough for the doctors to be concerned. I had additional symptoms with my kidneys and skin hives and was also diagnosed with asthma. I was put on the steroid prednisone for an extended period to calm things down.

It was used often with autoimmune diseases to decrease systemic inflammation. I felt *great* on the steroids. I had immense energy, and my brain fog lifted. One side effect for me was chipmunk cheeks.

I went to a family gathering, and my sister-in-law, who I hadn't seen in a while, was shocked to see me. I had the prednisone "moon face" and was still wearing a cast on my wrist. I looked worse than I felt, though. My mood was high from the steroids, and I remember feeling like they were happy pills. The fact that they decreased the inflammation in my body also positively affected my brain. I felt more focused and energetic than I had in a long time.

In 2004, after weaning off the extended dose of prednisone, I decided to do a marathon. It was on my bucket list, but it was the perfect time to do it to help me lose the weight I gained from being on steroids. I wanted to put my energy into something positive rather than being depressed that I had gained weight from the steroids.

I forgive myself for buying into the lie that I needed to do many things to be successful. The truth is that I get the most value in my life from the little moments spent with my family and friends, not from my success. Being present and enjoying those moments makes me happy and fills my life. Jesus says to "love others as much as yourself," and the more I love myself, the more I can love others. Self-love is the greatest gift I can give to others.

Chapter 7

Bouncing Back from More Trauma

The trauma in childhood had a significant impact on my development into adulthood. I was finally addressing the pain and wounds to feel capable and empowered. As a result, I was becoming more resilient and able to bounce back from other stressors. Unfortunately, I didn't realize that more trauma would come my way.

Losing a Sister

2001 was an eventful year for many reasons. I graduated with my Master's in Special Education from Lehigh University. I was studying to take the exam to become a Board-Certified Behavior Analyst (BCBA). Despite all the challenges that came my way, I succeeded in several areas of my life. Life was good!

In May of that same year, and only a few weeks after graduation, my sister Trish was diagnosed with inflammatory breast cancer. Trish was thirteen years older than me, and she was one of my safe people as a child. She was also in the car with us when the car accident happened in 1970. I had a different connection to her because of that.

I spent a lot of time with her because she was married and had two daughters who I was closer to in age than I was to Trish. When I had a panic attack triggered by something reminding me of the car accident, Trish was always there to make me feel safe. She also lived in the same town as I did. Like my oldest sister Paula, she was like a second mom to me. Paula lived in New Jersey, so I didn't spend much time with her in the years following the accident.

Trish had already had a biopsy and knew she had cancer at my graduation party. Still, she didn't tell any of us because she didn't want to ruin the celebration. So when she told us, I remember thinking everything was going to be all right. Our family was invincible since we had gotten through so much trauma before in our lives.

She went through chemotherapy, lost hair, and continued to be a pillar of strength. She was a model of resilience and had beaten cancer. Because it was such an aggressive form of cancer, her doctors recommended that she have a bilateral mastectomy to be safe and prevent it from returning. In October 2001, Trish underwent a mastectomy at. She was in the hospital for two days after the surgery to recover. I spoke to her on the phone, and her tone sounded optimistic. She was going home the next day, and things were finally turning the corner.

On the day, the day Trish was supposed to go home from the hospital, our world fell apart. I worked as a Behavior Specialist with a few clients at an early childhood education center between Easton and Bethlehem, Pennsylvania. My cell phone rang, and my sister Trish's husband Mitch was on the phone. He was upset and said Trish had gone into respiratory arrest earlier in the morning, and they had her on life support. He told me that I should get there as soon as possible.

My brain froze, and I did not fully realize what was happening at the time. I didn't even stop at my house to get anything, and I went directly to the hospital 90 minutes away. I arrived, and most of my siblings were there or on their way to the hospital. Trish's husband and children were all there too. Everyone was crying and comforting each other. We were all in shock at that moment. We didn't know for sure whether Trish would suffer permanent brain damage. Our oldest sister Paula is a nurse, and we waited until she arrived at the hospital so she could talk to the doctors to get more information and make any further decisions.

Paula arrived and conferred with the doctors about Trish's prognosis. She looked at the test results and communicated her findings with our family. The hospital was keeping her on life support so our family could say goodbye. Paula talked to Trish's husband, and their two oldest daughters to decide whether to take her off life support. Unfortunately, they made the difficult decision to remove her from life support as she had too much brain damage from lack of oxygen. Trish quietly passed away after we had our tearful and heartbreaking last moments with her.

Before this medical crisis, I wasn't as close to Trish as I lived away, and our lives were very different. She had four children and was living her life in Pennsylvania while I was in California and Florida. I didn't know it at the time—or I did—but I was messed up and wasn't in a good place to have a close relationship with any of my siblings. I was trying to survive, but I wasn't aware of that, let alone able to communicate that to others. My self-awareness was low until I started doing the challenging work of self-exploration. I moved back to Pennsylvania because I wanted to reconnect with my siblings. I was doing that, but I still felt disconnected from Trish. I still had a lot of shame that I needed to overcome. It was and sometimes still is a barrier in my relationships.

When I was diagnosed with social anxiety at the University of Pennsylvania Adult ADHD Center in 2014—more about this later—it didn't make sense initially. But on reflection, I realized the diagnosis fit. Social anxiety impacted my relationships, even with family members. I was so ashamed and didn't want them to see the real me. As I write this, I realize that it wasn't about what I did or didn't do but about what happened to me as a child and even as I got older. The trauma was insidious and clouded every aspect of my life.

I tried to connect with Trish a little more, but she had her family and a stepdaughter. She was trying to build a strong family. I respected her for doing that. I learned what it looks like to have a stepchild from both Trish and Paula, and they served as models for me once I became a stepparent.

Trish's death significantly affected her husband, children, grandchildren, our parents, siblings, and everyone else who interacted with her. I tried to be strong for her children, especially the two youngest, eleven and thirteen. Her two older daughters were married and were starting their own families. They stepped in as surrogate parents for the two youngest, and their strength continues to inspire me. I don't tell them often enough.

During the days after her death, I stayed at their house and slept with the youngest daughter, who was having trouble sleeping. I remembered that experience myself; when I was a child, I often found sleep difficult and woke up with panic attacks. I still had both of my parents, though, and I couldn't imagine what it was like to lose your mom unexpectedly. My heart broke for them more than anything. I didn't process my pain at that moment. It did, however, come up more as I did the work on myself through therapy and other self-discovery.

The viewing for Trish was incredible; lines of people wanting to share their condolences with us stretched around the block. Trish touched so many lives, and I had no idea. To this day, I still meet or talk to people she worked with in the past who talk about how amazing she was. No one could ever fill her shoes.

One of Trish and her husband's best friends gave the eulogy. I was in a fog that day at the church. It was packed with people, and I was sitting in the back, trying to catch my breath. The shock started to wear off, and I was uncomfortable with the emotions it was bringing up for me. I was only at the beginning of my healing journey, and the band-aid was slowly coming off to reveal the genuine wounds.

> *I forgive myself for buying into the lie that I will have the chance to spend time with the people I love once I am successful. The truth is that I wasted too much time away from family and friends while focusing on success. We don't know when someone will be taken from us, and we must cherish every minute and be present in those little moments.*

Chapter 8

Success Begins to Take Hold for Now

When I graduated from Lehigh University in 2001 with my master's degree, the excitement made me feel like a real adult, and I was finally settling into it. I thought, *this is it…I finally made it!* I was thirty-six years old and felt like my life was beginning to manifest my vision. I had a graduation party and felt like I had something to celebrate. The party was at my house, and I made two of my favorite vegetarian foods, my mom's haluski recipe and black bean burritos. I was hosting my family and friends for the first time in my life for a festive event. My self-worth was the highest it had ever been and was all tied to my accomplishments.

My first job was as a Behavior Specialist Consultant for a behavioral health agency in the Lehigh Valley right out of school. I worked primarily with children with autism spectrum disorders. I was naturally good at this work and deeply connected with the children. Even though some of them couldn't talk with their voice, they spoke to me through a deep connection between individuals who had been through difficult times at a very young age. I felt like I was in their shoes whenever I heard an adult treated them inappropriately. I was so in tune with their triggers that I didn't realize they were also my triggers. One way my PTSD showed up was to be a mama bear. I became a fierce advocate for children and adults with disabilities. I knew I was in the right field of work if I didn't let it get the best of me. It never did.

I was good at my job. I had great relationships with the children, their families, and my colleagues. My boss even asked me to do training for other behavior specialists and mobile therapists on applied behavior analysis and other key concepts of our work. It made me feel good about myself, and my confidence grew.

I was studying for the exam to become a Board-Certified Behavior Analyst, which was the final hurdle to making my dream career a reality. On the second try, I passed and made it official. It took eight years from when I decided I wanted to be a behavior analyst until it came true.

I was a voracious student of learning for my work. I wanted to learn everything that I could. So I went to workshops, and one of the first ones I went to was on verbal behavior with Mark Sundberg. I fell in love with it and went to every workshop I could. I attended an intensive verbal behavior workshop with Vince Carbone in Brick Township, New Jersey. That's where I met Mary and Brenda. They were behavior specialists from an area in Pennsylvania near me, and we immediately hit it off. We were on the same career paths and connected on many levels. So we had a great time, and I learned a ton.

About six months after the training, Mary reached out to me and asked if I would be interested in being a Senior Consultant for the Pennsylvania Verbal Behavior Project starting in Pennsylvania. It was a partnership between the Pennsylvania Training and Technical Assistance Network (PaTTAN) and Supporting Autism and Families Everywhere (S.A.F.E.). It was a part-time job, so I could keep doing my other full-time work. I was assigned to a classroom about an hour from my house, so I had a pleasant little commute once per week. I liked driving, so I didn't mind the commute—being a passenger in a car was a different story.

> *I forgive myself for buying into the lie that I do not have much to offer, and others must have errors in judgment if they want to work with or spend time with me. The truth is that my story and gifts are worth sharing. I have empathy for people who cannot advocate for themselves, and I need to trust that empathy as it guides me in my life. The adversity in my life has given me insight into others and ignites the passion inside me to fight for them.*

Chapter 9

Healing and Closure

After Trish died in 2001, I spent even more time with my parents in the house where we all grew up. My dad and I had a much better relationship than when I was a child. He often told me that he blamed himself for everything I went through as a child. He had been retired from his work for several years, and he spent time doing odd projects around the house while I lived away. He was doing much less woodworking as his health had deteriorated. So he and my mom spent their time together enjoying retirement and living a more peaceful life than ever.

My dad was now willing to talk about things that were difficult to talk about when I was a child. He also respected me more because of my arduous work and accomplishments. I could say things to my dad that my other siblings couldn't say to him. Since I was single and had a successful career, I could spend time with my parents and visit them often. I cut his hair and gave him a good shave at their house. We watched TV and movies and talked about life in general. He admitted that he could have handled being a parent better. He was only doing what he knew. He shared stories with me about his childhood and how he felt bullied by his older brother. I also think that after losing Trish, both parents had even more urgency to spend time with their children and grandchildren. Nothing was guaranteed, and he knew his life was getting shorter by the day. Unfortunately, his health hadn't been good in years, slowly worsening.

In 2003, my dad's health deteriorated. In 1996 he suffered from a bleeding ulcer and had surgery to remove a sizable portion of his stomach. He had high blood pressure and high cholesterol for several years. He wasn't active and continued to drink beer regularly and smoke cigarettes on a limited basis. He hadn't smoked in the house for several years since new research came out on second-hand smoke. He was old for the seventy-six years he lived.

In October, my dad's health put him in the hospital. He was belligerent and combative with the nurses and doctors. This behavior wasn't typical for him, as he was traditionally always very cordial with people outside our home. Our mom told us not to come to see him because his moods were incredibly stressful for the family. She always tried to protect us, even if she didn't have the tools to do it. My sister Lisa was at the hospital as she lived nearby our parents.

His health turned critical, and they planned to life-flight him to Hershey Medical Center to give him better care. The local hospital didn't know what was wrong with him and felt Hershey could do a better job. So I told my mom I would go as she needed to rest and care for herself.

I called my oldest sister Paula and told her I was headed to the hospital in Hershey. She lived in New Jersey and planned to meet me there as soon as possible. I got to the hospital in the early afternoon, just after he arrived. My dad was barely conscious and on life-support, and it was hard to see him that way. He was intubated and couldn't talk to me. We couldn't talk, but his eyes spoke as much as they could. He was agitated from having all the tubes and wires hooked up. He didn't like being in the hospital, which was his worst scenario. His voice was silenced because of the tubes down his throat, which was hard for him.

The doctors and nurses did everything they could but had no answers for what was wrong with him. They thought he may have had a stroke. His health was failing quickly, yet I felt connected to him during these hours. I tried to calm him down and prayed with him. He was less agitated as I did this. He looked deep into my eyes once and seemed to communicate, "let me go." I felt it very strongly, yet I was at peace with it.

Our relationship had improved over the years, and I had forgiven him for how he treated me. God gave me the gift of mercy, and that was the best gift I could want. It freed me from holding onto the pain that I had already processed. I empathized with my dad and realized that he and my mom did their best with their skills. We had the shared experience of being the youngest of our families. Even with the barriers between us over the years, the accident created a bond that was intangible but present.

My sister Paula got to the hospital later that evening. We comforted our dad and let him get some rest. Again, Paula's nursing skills helped us get the details we needed from the doctors. They told us to leave and get some rest after we stayed until late in the night. So we checked into our hotel and caught up on things.

Our mom and other siblings came to the hospital the next day. Dad was still not very awake. He was heavily medicated, and they were keeping him comfortable. Later in the afternoon, a few family members were in the room with him; he was no longer intubated and could speak more coherently. Briefly, he said he was happy to see us. We were encouraged by this, but we knew he wasn't in the best shape. Then, about an hour later, the doctors told us he passed away not long after he spoke for the last time.

I was very much at peace with my dad's death. My faith comforted me, unlike any other loss in my life. God the Father was with me in full force to fill the hole of my broken childhood relationship with my dad and comfort me with the loss. I knew my dad was finally at peace, and any pain he caused was gone with him. He suffered so much over his life, and I was happy he no longer suffered, physically and emotionally.

I cried extraordinarily little during this time. I didn't know if I was numb or just at peace with my dad's passing. My faith gave me the strength to know that I was not alone and that I needed to grow from my relationship with my dad, even the bad parts of it. Our family was together, and we focused on supporting our mom, though we knew she would be fine. Her faith and personality were her strength, and she would never be alone.

I forgive myself for buying into the lie that my dad did not care about me. The truth is that he had been through his own pain, and I cherish who he became because of that pain, both the good and bad. As an adult, I understand my dad so much more and do not doubt that he lived with the guilt that he caused much of my pain as a child. He often told me as much, but he did not need to carry that guilt. It was a blessing for me to be with him at his death and break the self-imposed chains he put on himself.

$Chapter$ 10

Taking Steps Forward

Disney Marathon—Party at the Hospital

I continued the exercise and training I had done my entire life, but I had a different purpose for it now. It wasn't just to keep me looking good on the outside but to keep my body from self-destructing with autoimmune issues. I ran about fifteen to twenty miles a week, rode my bike about thirty miles a week, and swam at the pool two days a week. I was lean, living on a vegetarian diet, and not drinking any alcohol. I felt good about myself. My emotions were still raw at times and living on the surface, but I felt like I was finally dealing with the pain I had tried to cover up so often. I wasn't self-medicating, at least not with things damaging to me. So I started signing up for local races like I had done while living in California. Those events have continuously fed me and empowered me to keep going and push myself farther.

In the Summer of 2004, I participated in a 10K race in the Lehigh Valley. I met someone who was a coach for Team in Training (TNT). TNT is the Leukemia & Lymphoma Society's team to coach individuals to complete a half marathon, marathon, triathlon, or bike race to raise money in honor of or in memory of someone with blood cancer.

I signed up to do the Disney Marathon in January 2004. We trained as a group and had a coach guide us along the way. The experience was unique and encouraged me to complete a marathon with a team of people. We all supported each other along the way and had many people cheering us on during the race. It was like a fraternity, as you would hear shouts of "go, team" throughout the race. I'm not sure I would have done the marathon without the support. Raising money for a worthy cause was a bonus.

I did everything right to prepare for the race. I trained with my team doing longer and longer runs on alternating weekends. I ran the rest of the prescribed training plan alone or with the team. I had been doing it right, yet I still questioned whether I had what it took to finish a marathon. The imposter syndrome that plagued me my entire life was trying to take over again. I was still afraid to let people see the real me and instead focused on my goal. I told myself not to show any weakness because I felt people would leave me if I appeared weak.

The week before the race, we ran shorter runs. This gave my body a rest and helped it prepare for the longest race of my life. Excitement started boiling once we traveled to the airport to catch our flight to Orlando, Florida. My body experienced both excitement and anxiety, but I didn't recognize the difference at this point. It wasn't until much later that I could identify my symptoms and triggers.

We arrived at the Disney property, and we settled into our hotels. The atmosphere was electric, and our team was together. Many fun activities helped prepare us for the race—various celebrations and plenty of pasta for carb loading. I did the ritual of downing a plate full of carbs the night before a race, and it felt good not to think about holding back.

We all tried to go to bed as early as we could, but the excitement made it hard to do. I finally went to bed at about 10 p.m., and we had to wake up a 3 a.m. to get shuttled to the starting line. The morning of the race was cold by Florida's standards. Everything was in place as it was supposed to be.

I hydrated with electrolytes the day before and during the race. I wore layers of clothes since it was thirty-eight degrees while we were waiting to start the race early in the morning. We had throw-away clothes so we wouldn't have to carry them once we dropped a layer as the temperature increased. I had prepared myself physically and mentally as best I could have. We used the Galloway method of completing a marathon by running for three minutes and walking for one minute. It is helpful for beginners and decreases your risk of injury. After the first few miles, the butterflies in my stomach subsided, and I was excited by all the people cheering us along the marathon route, "go, team!" People were dressed in purple—the TNT colors—and our fraternity grew even more prominent as the race continued. Bands and other forms of entertainment encouraged us at every mile marker. Disney knows how to put on a race, and I was so excited that this is where I chose to do my first-ever marathon.

I did great for most of the race, but I started hitting a wall around mile twenty-three. I slowed down even more than I had done previously. My coach, Gary, stayed with me to cross the finish line. I crossed, and it was a fantastic feeling of accomplishment. Unfortunately, that feeling didn't last long, as I became dizzy. My coach took me into the medical tent to get checked out. My blood pressure dropped to 70/40. They put me on a cot, and my blood pressure still did not rise. After ten minutes, they took me to the hospital in an ambulance. I spent the rest of the day in the emergency room as they gave me intravenous fluids and ran some tests. One test for blood clots in your lungs, the D-Dimer test, was positive. They X-rayed my chest to look for a blood clot in my lungs. The X-ray was negative, so they continued IV fluids and kept an eye on me. I remained in the hospital the entire day with my coach by my side and was finally discharged at about seven that evening. I missed most of the post-marathon celebrations with my team. I was exhausted and starving because I didn't get to eat anything other than crackers until 8:00 p.m., but I still felt a sense of accomplishment.

My teammates kept coming to my room and checking up on me, and I was grateful for all the support. Mentally and emotionally, it was just "another thing to go through" in my life. My early childhood trauma gave me one positive thing, resilience. I didn't let the fact that I ended up in the hospital take away from the fact that I finished running twenty-six miles in one day!

On the outside, I looked like I had taken the whole thing in stride. On the inside, that loud and roaring voice yelled at me, saying I would never be okay and would always screw something up. I didn't know it then, but the critical inner voice was trying to take away my triumph. I had excuses for why I didn't finish the race in under five hours—5:20 was my actual time. I struggled to accept what happened and credit myself for finishing something unique. The habitual negative self-talk took over and once again overwhelmed any good in my life. I just put on a brave face, tried to push through, and went on to the next race.

Pacific Crest Triathlon—Overcoming Glaciers, Mountains, and Flat Tires

I couldn't let myself rest. I needed to prove that I could finish something substantial again. I signed up for another event through Team In Training. This time, it was an Olympic Distance triathlon in Bend, Oregon. I loved triathlons because they kept my ADHD brain from getting bored. I had trained for triathlons when I lived in Florida and even did open water swims near Clearwater Beach in the Gulf of Mexico. I felt like I was already prepared and wouldn't crash as I did for the marathon. No more trips to the hospital after a race!

The training for the marathon helped prepare me for the triathlon. I met a few new friends and trained with other friends I met and knew well through the Disney marathon. I felt like I was part of a tribe and proud of it. But deep down, even though

I didn't know it, I still didn't think I deserved to have a great life. I was not as needy for approval as I was earlier in my life, but a level of shame about myself lurked hidden underneath all the success.

I was looking for someone to spend my life with as I got older. I subtly looked at guys as potential relationship material, but I was much more confident in who I was after doing some work on myself. I met guys through Team In Training, but I was happy to have them as friends rather than being in a relationship with them. I wanted to be myself with people and not feel like I had to prove something. My need for approval from others lessened but didn't go away completely. I still desire some level of approval, as long as it doesn't interfere with me asking for my needs to be met.

The day came for us to go to Bend, Oregon, for the race. I was excited to go to the Pacific Crest triathlon weekend. I hadn't been to Oregon in several years and couldn't wait to return to the West Coast again. Oregon especially felt like "me." So I drove in my Saab with the sunroof open and blasting my motivational playlist to get in the zone as I drove to the Philly airport. "Get up, Stand up" by Bob Marley was blasting as I sang along. Music has always played a significant role in my life; its influence fueled my excitement. Other artists on my playlist were Mary J. Blige, Santana, and Bob Marley. For some reason I don't remember, I chose to drive on my own to the airport.

At the airport, I met my teammates. We traveled with the Lehigh Valley chapter and Philadelphia chapter TNT teams for the Half-IRONMAN triathlon and the Olympic Distance triathlons. Our group was large. Our bikes and gear were shipped before we traveled, so we only carried personal items and clothes.

We landed in Portland after dark and took a bus to Bend. We couldn't see the beautiful scenery on our drive, and I couldn't wrap my head around where we were. I was always a little "side seat driver" and was good at remembering places we've been or were going. I'm unsure if that was because of the car accident or something else.

Our team stayed at the Sunriver Resort in Bend, Oregon, and when we arrived, we went directly to our rooms and to sleep. Our accommodation was a set of lovely townhouses. We traveled several days before the race, so the people doing the Half-IRONMAN race had enough time to acclimate to the elevation. Their race was before ours, so we had a little extra time to kick around Bend.

I became good friends with two teammates, Brianna, and Susan, and we hung out for the entire trip. I suggested we go whitewater rafting as there were some excellent rivers in the area. Susan was a raft guide on the Lehigh River in Pennsylvania, so this was cake for her. I had rafted on the South Fork of the American River in California when I worked at a health club while living in the San Francisco Bay area. We took trips with a group from the club and had such a blast. That was my first experience with whitewater rafting, and it was Class IV.

We went on the Deschutes River near Bend. It was a short trip since we didn't want to get too tired before the race, but it was a lot of fun. A big festival was associated with the Pacific Crest triathlon, so we found plenty of other things to do.

The Half-IRONMAN triathlon race came first, and we cheered on our teammates. We couldn't go out to the race start because of limited transportation, but we cheered them on at the finish line. I had always dreamed of doing an IRONMAN triathlon, so I was inspired by my teammates, and it was great to see them do so well!

The day of our race finally came. I was nervous and excited at the same time. We took our bikes out the day before and had everything set up for the swim-to-bike transition. I listened to my motivational playlist to calm my mind before the race during the bus ride to the starting line.

The course was beautiful, and the swim portion of the race was in a glacier-fed lake. I had swum in open water many times when I lived in Florida, but I had never worn a wetsuit for a swim before. I put the suit on, which was tight to reduce drag. I didn't think the suit would significantly affect how I felt during the race. I was ready to go and felt confident I would do well during the swim.

Before the race began, I wanted to test the water, so I jumped in to get comfortable with the temperature. It was freezing cold and took my breath away. I had grown up swimming at Knoebels Grove Amusement Park in Elysburg, Pennsylvania. Swimming was one of my strengths, and it's not usually a strength for most people doing a triathlon. My comfort with swimming took away some of the stress for the race, but that quickly changed in a glacier-fed lake while wearing a tight triathlon wetsuit.

The starting gun sounded, and 150 of us jumped in and started swimming. It was like a group of salmon swimming upstream as we were all on top of each other. It was hard to swim without bumping into someone. When I put my head down, I could barely hold my breath. The wetsuit felt constricting on my lungs, and the elevation added to the swim challenge.

The swim length was nine-tenths of a mile, and the course ran in a big diamond shape to the middle of the lake. It was the most challenging swim I have ever done. I couldn't catch my breath and felt like I was experiencing a panic attack. For a while, I ended up on my back and tried to stay on course. Eventually, I settled down enough so I could switch between swimming on my back and face down. It was disconcerting to have such a tough time with a swim. It took me off guard. I was tempted to quit right at the beginning of the race, and swimming was my strength! My confidence took a big hit, but I was determined to keep going.

We finished the swim and got to our bikes. We all talked about how rough the swim was for us. I felt better, realizing that I wasn't the only one struggling. We had to take our wetsuits off and put on our cycling shoes. I had a tough time getting the wetsuit off and had to get help from a teammate.

We all started on the bike portion together. Out of the constricting wetsuit, I could breathe better again, raising my spirits. The wetsuit threw me for a loop, and I needed to get my head back in racing gear. I was with my teammates Brianna and Susan, my friends and training partners. It felt good to be racing with them.

Leading up to the race, I was worried that I did not have a backup tire for my bike. It was a vintage Tomassini ten-speed racing bike that was restored to mint condition by a friend. The tires were glue-in, so they didn't have inner tubes. If your tire became flat or damaged, it needed to be replaced. I didn't think about anything happening as I had ridden this bike for years without any issues.

The days before the race, we looked around the town and resort, but I couldn't find a glue-in tire. I was just going to have to take my chances. The course was all on asphalt, so I thought it wouldn't be an issue.

The Cascade mountains of Central Oregon are beautiful, and they reminded me of Pennsylvania in some ways, but much more extensive. The triathlon cycling course had some rolling hills with some steep climbs and drops. It was tough but felt doable after the harrowing experience with the swim.

We were going up a steep hill at about mile sixteen of the bike portion of the race. We were about halfway through the biking portion, and I felt good about my pace and stamina. Then, I began to feel like I had concrete on my feet. The hill was kicking my butt suddenly. I stopped to check out my bike; of course, I had a flat tire. The rubber was still glued to the rim and was intact on the bike; I had no way to fix the flat. Brianna and Susan said they would quickly race to the finish line to get me help. I planned to walk with my bike until someone returned for me. They raced on, and I hydrated up, so I didn't crash as I walked those hills. I watched them go ahead and felt my emotions start to roil. I was bummed that I wouldn't be able to finish the race after all that hard work. It felt like it was all over.

About a mile after my flat tire, I reached the top of the mountain. The previous portion of the road was the most challenging part of the bike course, and the rest was downhill or flat. I decided to try coasting with my bike. The rubber tire was still completely intact on the rim and offered enough cushion to make it worth trying. I started slowly coasting down the hill. As I rolled forward, my hopes began to rise; I realized I wouldn't be stuck in the middle of the Oregon mountains by myself. It turns out the photographers took my picture while I was riding my bike; you can't even tell I had a flat.

The last several miles of the bike portion flattened out as the route transitioned to the run. I was going at a good pace considering the condition of my bike. I kept my head down and focused on getting to the next stop. A few people passed me, but not too many. I felt good that I was still fighting.

On the other side of the road, I saw someone riding a bike and carrying an entire bike wheel in one hand. He was headed up the mountain, the direction I just came from. It was our coach. It didn't register that my teammates were looking for me. I didn't train with him much, as he was from the Philly chapter, but he was an accomplished triathlete. My brain was in the zone, and I didn't think to yell at him. I thought he was going for something else. I also thought he may have seen me and would turn around.

About twenty minutes later, I made it to the transition from the bike to the run. The race's final stretch was a 10K run and an easy course. When I got to the bike drop-off, some teammates told me that one of the coaches was riding to take the wheel for me. I was so used to doing things on my own, so I couldn't fathom that someone was doing all that to help *me*. I was grateful.

I ran the 10K with a few other teammates. Brianna and Susan had already finished and were cheering me on as I neared the finish line of the entire race. They couldn't believe I was still racing and about to finish the complete triathlon. They mauled me when I crossed the finish line and told me how amazing I was to finish the bike ride on a flat tire and keep going after that. I felt relief and a tremendous sense of accomplishment. The day ended with a heartwarming and satisfying team celebration dinner after the race.

For most of my life, I've felt I had to do everything myself and that if I asked for help, I would be rejected. Experiencing people who cared about me and had my back was foreign. My parents would be there for me if I needed help as a child, but the emotion was lacking. I always felt spoiled because my siblings told me I was. As an adult, I realized I wasn't spoiled as a child. I didn't have consistent parenting, which made it look like I got away with murder and didn't have to do some of the things my older siblings had to do regarding responsibilities and freedoms.

One time when I was complimenting my oldest sister for her beautiful handwriting, she said that it was because dad worked with her a lot so she wouldn't have the lousy handwriting he did. Having our dad help with homework was a foreign concept to me. He *never* helped me with homework or attended my sporting events. I always had to go to him and do what he was doing if I wanted to spend time with him. This lack of interest in me triggered me to lower my expectations of others.

Doing the marathon and triathlon with the Leukemia & Lymphoma Society's Team In Training gave me a strong group of people to bond with, supporting me to do things I couldn't have done myself. They helped me reach my goals and accomplish some things on my bucket list. I learned that I could trust people a little more, and my guard started to come down.

> *I forgive myself for buying into the lie that I need to do things on my own to prove my worth. The truth is that I have a team of people who love and care for me to get me through any difficulty. I can do much more when I collaborate with others and work as a team rather than isolating myself. I just must let them help me.*

Chapter 11

Success in Old Places

In 2003, my career started to take off. I was working as an educational consultant for behavior and autism at a state office that provides training and technical assistance for school districts and intermediate units in Pennsylvania. I loved the work and the people I worked with on this critical path. We were doing innovative things and were on the forefront of growth and learning in education. I loved this job and could see myself working there for the rest of my career.

I was working in the central region of Pennsylvania and lived in the eastern region, which was about an hour and ten minutes' drive each way to my office. I didn't mind and loved listening to music on the trip. Listening to music was one of my relaxing self-care activities, but I didn't understand self-care at the time. It was just something I liked. We have learned much more about trauma, and how positive, protective factors can build resilience in people.

Music was both an escape and a calming activity for me. My identity is very connected to specific music, making me feel a deeper connection to my soul when I play those songs. Mary J Blige, Erykah Badu, Aaliyah, and Jill Scott were some artists who made me feel strong and free. I also listened to Electric Light Orchestra (ELO), Steely Dan, the Doobie Brothers,

Huey Lewis and the News, Joni Mitchell, Crosby, Stills, Nash & Young, George Benson, Marvin Gaye, the Indigo Girls, Jodeci, and many more. My eclectic music selections reflected my complicated personality and were influential healing factors throughout my life.

I spent many weekends in the Catskills of New York at a meditation retreat center between 1999-2005. It was part of the work I did on healing my inner trauma and pain that had accumulated for over thirty years. The meditation was a gift that strengthened my faith and healed my emotional pain. It was not tied to any religion but strengthened my connection with God to a level I hadn't experienced before. I woke up every morning at 4:00 a. m. to meditate before work and school and again in the evening to keep myself grounded. I had routines of meditation, a healthy vegetarian diet, and exercise that created a solid foundation of peace and healing.

My self-esteem was on a straight track upwards, and I continued to gain strength as I maintained my routines. I felt more whole than I could have imagined. The consistency of these things made it easy for me to build solid habits, and I didn't have to overthink what I was doing. The routines became automatic and allowed me to strengthen my relationships with family and new friends. My anxiety was at an all-time low, though I was still taking medication. I was at peace with taking medication because trauma and mental health issues are like any other illness that needs to be treated based on the symptoms at the moment.

My work took me to locations in central Pennsylvania I had never visited before. I gained an appreciation of Pennsylvania I didn't have as a child. I didn't know what a beautiful treasure I had in my backyard. I loved traveling around Pennsylvania and meeting new people as I worked in schools to support teachers and other staff in managing student behaviors.

The work I was doing also brought up some old wounds. Working in schools with children with significant behavior problems reminded me of my childhood struggles. I internalized my trauma and hid it behind a mask, and these kids wore a different kind of mask. The outside world saw some of the worst in their negative behaviors. Their true self was hidden behind the behaviors which were the first thing people saw. The shining souls of these children and adults I worked with were buried deep like a diamond in a piece of coal. I wanted to help the adults who worked with them to see the real gem behind their behaviors. When adults couldn't see that, it sometimes triggered me emotionally. It took me right back to my childhood when people made assumptions about me because of my panic attacks or how I looked.

I got the kids and knew I could help them most by supporting the adults who worked with them. If I could prevent one child from going through what I went through as a child, it was all worth it. I continued to grow and learn about myself as I gained more experience with work. I was a learning sponge, and it gave me more strength. It also helped me feel a bit more in control. I could always learn, and that was definitely a choice within my control. No one could take away the knowledge I gained about how to support children with more intensive needs.

I forgive myself for buying into the lie that I would be fixed overnight by finally getting help for my trauma. The truth is that healing is a process that takes time, and it may ebb and flow at various times in my life. It is okay to be affected by reminders of my trauma. I cannot expect to be immune to pain and adversity. My coping skills, self-worth, and relationship with Jesus get me through challenging times now and for the rest of my life.

Chapter 12

Headed Home

My work often took me to the area where I grew up and allowed me to spend more time with my mom. She still lived in the house where we all grew up, and I stayed there if I had to work multiple days in the area or if I had to travel further north. I loved having so much one-on-one time with my mom and being back home often.

My sister Lisa and her family lived fifteen minutes from my mom and close to Knoebels Amusement Park, where we grew up and where I had so many beautiful memories. Their house was a perfect little cape cod in a sleepy part of town. It fit their family like a glove and created a sanctuary for them. When I found out the cost of houses in the area, I realized I could buy a house there too. The thought of taking this step was exciting and scary. I would be moving back home to where I grew up and to all the good and bad memories. Was I kidding myself to think I could do this and be okay? No, it was the right time to do it, and I felt stronger to handle any memories.

In 2005, after commuting an hour each way for three years, I sold my house in three days at the peak of the housing boom for a healthy profit. The quick sale made it easier to plan my move back to the hometown area I had been away from for eighteen years. I didn't have a new house and had to move into my childhood home and stay with my mom until I found one.

This time with my mom was so precious. We already had a strong relationship as she was my safe person but staying with her at this time in my life took it to a new level. I wasn't afraid to push her to talk about things, but I made it safe for her to process her pain about my childhood. I told her I was stronger because of everything the adversities I overcame. She was my buddy, and I was the same for her. We did a lot of things together and enjoyed being roommates again. I look back on this time as evidence of my healing. It was so great to be back home again.

I talked about the car accident increasingly with my family. Not only was I more comfortable talking about it, but they were too. My oldest sister Paula told me about some of her experiences during the car accident that changed our lives. She was in nursing school then and stayed with mom at our aunt's house near the hospital. She vowed never to work in a hospital that had a policy that parents could not stay with their children while they were in the hospital. The damage to me was apparent and would be something that would stay with me for the rest of my life. I did not understand how it also impacted my family.

My mom and I had more in-depth conversations, and she felt more comfortable talking about the accident as well. It pained her, and she shared how it pained my dad for the rest of his life. He told me that he had always blamed himself for the accident, but I could see it more for myself. This time was a wonderful time of further healing. I learned that hiding things, even from many years ago, was not helping. If I was going to heal the wounds of my childhood trauma, I needed to be transparent and help other family members heal by making it safe for them to talk.

While staying at my mom's house, I also looked for a home to purchase. Most of my worldly things were in a storage unit five minutes away. It was comfortable living in my childhood home, but I was ready to be in my place. I started looking at houses in the tiny hamlet in a beautiful valley. Mountains rose sharply on both sides of the valley floor. This area was mostly farmland when I was a child and had a small cluster of lovely homes throughout the central part of the small town. Many friends lived in this area, so it always felt like home to me.

I felt like I was starting a significant new chapter in my life. I turned forty years old in 2006 and was excited to begin my life anew with a fresh perspective of myself and how I wanted to live my life. The old perspective of prioritizing looking good and hiding the real me was not something I wanted to take into this new phase of my life—that included my job, home, social life, spiritual life, and everything else. To some degree, I wanted to bury who I'd been in past relationships and shine forth the parts of myself I was proud of that served me well. My career was already moving positively, and I felt like I had a purpose bigger than me slowly coming out. How my childhood trauma would influence this new life wasn't clear then, but I knew that I was ready for a new adventure and was open to the unknown in my future.

My sister Lisa had found their house through friends from her ministry with women. It was in the family for many years, and they wanted someone who could appreciate the history to live in their family home. When I was looking for a house, the same family was about to sell a place about one mile up the road from my sister's house. The two women who lived in each house were best friends and spent many years living close to each other like sisters. Betsy, who previously owned my sister's house, had passed away. Grace, who owned the other home, was in a nursing facility in her nineties with failing health. So the family decided to sell the property when her health further declined.

One day, Lisa called me and told me Grace's family was at the house. I was excited to hear more about it and see the house. I knew the story of how the two women were like sisters and traveled the country and the world together. Lisa connected me with the family, and I went to see the house. As soon as I saw the front of the house and the property, I knew it would be my forever home. It needed significant work, but the bones and the perfect location were incredible. It was a brown ranch home sitting on a beautiful acre-and-a-quarter property with a lot of natural landscaping. It was late February when I looked at the house, but I could see the dogwood trees and sizeable single-story-sized rhododendrons sprinkling the property. Most of the property had large trees of all kinds. It felt like a lodge, and I could envision myself living there.

As I walked into the house to the living room, the first thing that caught my eye was the large floor-to-ceiling windows looking over the back deck and pool area. The pool was covered, and the day was gray with clouds and a cold breeze. It was kidney-shaped, and I could imagine having family gatherings with swimming and entertaining on the large deck. The living room had cathedral ceilings with large wooden beams ending at the large brick fireplace that was the room's centerpiece. I was sold. The family was thrilled to have two sisters buy the houses of their family members to keep the atmosphere alive. Grace had never married and lived in the house alone, yet she always invited people to come and swim in her pool. She loved to entertain, and it just happened that I did too. It was perfect.

Finally, Feeling Worth a Relationship

I started to plan for the mortgage, packed up my things, and took care of all that needed to be done before I moved into my new home. I was ready to meet some new people further to kick off the new decade of my life. So I decided to check out online dating sources to see if I could meet new people in the area. Online dating had just started to take off in the early 2000s, and I knew other friends who had been successful with it.

I had not dated anyone in over six years, and I had changed considerably during that time. I had done a lot of inner work and felt more confident in who I was and what I had to offer in relationships. I was very gun-shy and just wanted to find someone to hang out with for some new adventures. I tried eHarmony and was unsuccessful in meeting anyone I was interested in then. My dating standards had increased significantly, and I was not afraid to be fussy. I felt like I finally deserved to have a good relationship in my life, and I was content being single. I was not looking for anyone to fill my life, just someone who would be a friend to start. If it did not go anywhere, I was okay with that. I had already made peace with being single for the rest of my life and not having any children. I had nothing to lose and plenty of patience to spare.

I shared my lack of dating adventures with two friends I became close with through work. They were like a big brother and big sister to me. Ruth suggested I go on match.com and try that online dating site out. I did, and it was much easier to see what was out there. It felt like shopping for shoes but with people. I could easily find someone with similar interests, and I was open to dating guys I would not have considered dating before because of my low self-esteem. I knew that I deserved to have a good guy and a better relationship in my life. This dating experience was the first time in my entire life that I had this realization. It felt good to be the real me, and I was more than enough for someone else. So I did not need to put on a show or hide who I was in my profile.

One day, as I was checking the site, one guy looked at my profile and sent me a notification. He did not reach out to me. He just "looked" at my profile. I looked at his profile, and it piqued my interest. Mark was a white, single dad with two children aged sixteen and eighteen. He was handsome and active with whitewater kayaking. Pictures of his adventures filled his profile, and I liked his self-portrayal. He talked about how much he loved his children, being a dad, and still believed in marriage even though he had been divorced.

Meeting someone online was out of my comfort zone, but I was willing to take a risk and had nothing to lose. I "winked" at Mark on the dating platform, opening the door for us to talk. So we scheduled a time to talk the day after my fortieth birthday. I remember the call so clearly. I was nervous, like a teenager waiting for a boy to call for the first time. I was still staying with my mom and was packing to get ready to move to my new house a week later. So taking the call in the bedroom where I grew up made me feel even more like a teenager.

I picked up the phone after a few rings, and his voice was strong and gentle at the same time. We spoke for about thirty minutes, and it was surprisingly easy. It was light and very natural. He had a big job to do the next day, so we did not talk for too long. So we scheduled a time to talk the following evening. That was the beginning of two weeks of almost nightly two- to three-hour phone conversations before we could meet in person. Our face-to-face meeting was delayed because I was moving into my new house, and he went to a long weekend kayak whitewater festival.

We talked about everything from family to adventures, from work to places we lived, and from relationships to dreams for our future. We joke now that he was interrogating me because he had been through so much in his previous relationships. He wanted to ensure I had no surprise baggage in my closet. At least my baggage was not as heavy as it was seven years before we met. I told him that I was looking for friendship at this point, but he knew already that it was going farther than just friendship. We both did, but it made me feel better to say it anyway. I did not grow up knowing how to set boundaries, and I was exercising my newly learned skills. He offered to help me move, but I declined his offer. I was not ready to show the slightly stressed side of me and thought it would be too much to move into a new house *and* simultaneously meet a new romantic interest.

He had some of his own baggage, but that would be discovered later. We do not always realize how things impact us until we are way past the incidents. That is the insidiousness of trauma—we often do not know its long-term effects as they can be quite subtle. It is like a drop of water in a bucket that fills up without us knowing that it was even raining in the first place.

We finally had our first date two weeks after our first conversation. We were going whitewater paddling on the Lehigh River at the end of April. The road into his house was long, windy, and set in the beautiful hills across the river from Danville. I pulled into the driveway of his quaint house, sitting back on the upper side of a hollow. Various kinds of boats were sitting around the property; it looked like an adventure house. He came outside to meet me, and my stomach had a few butterflies. It was different this time. I felt more comfortable with myself and was not afraid to be me. I also felt wonderfully comfortable with him because we had spent so much time talking on the phone in the weeks leading up to our first in-person meeting.

He was much more handsome in person than his pictures portrayed. I felt like I was meeting a long-lost friend for the first time. It was exciting, comfortable, and felt very real. For the first time in my life, I felt like I was showing another person the real me. I was more confident that I was worthy of having someone in my life who treated me well. I was not afraid to set that boundary *and* let someone into the dark parts of my life. I was not hiding anything from him. That was a new experience, and it was very freeing.

I went into his house, and his son Nathan was there. He was a handsome sixteen-year-old boy who had his dad's charismatic personality. The first thing he did was bust on me. He said, "so you're a vegetarian." I laughed and said, "yes." I was used to people teasing me since I was the youngest in my family. It has always been a sign that someone felt comfortable with me enough to tease me. Nathan was a sweet kid, and I knew we would have a good relationship. I did not know much we had in common, but it felt like we knew each other more than we realized.

The house looked like a single-dad's house with some older furniture, a gym in the living room, and lots of stuff lying around. It felt like a grown adult's fraternity house, but that did not intimidate me in any way. I could see who he was underneath the outside dressings. He was a single dad of two who knew who he was and was not afraid to show it. His relationship with his kids was natural; I loved that about him. Nothing was going to scare me away, and I had no reason to fear what was coming. It was our first date, after all. I did not need to overanalyze anything and was happy to be comfortable at the moment.

We packed up his truck and had all the gear we needed. On the way to the river, I had to stop and get a few band-aids at the pharmacy to cover up my few cuts from moving into my new house. I walked into the pharmacy, and my nephew Mick was working that day. I asked to use the bathroom and went to the back of the store as I left Mick and Mark to talk. Sometime later, Mark told me what Mick had said to him. He said, "If you and my Aunt Anne get married, I'll be your nephew." *Ugh*! It was par for Mick as he was a tender-hearted and candid teenage boy. He was happy to meet someone I was finally dating. My dating was a foreign experience for him since I had not dated for seven years and had lived in Florida before that. He had only met one boyfriend before, so this was new. So, I got the band-aids, and we left to go to the river.

It was not the warmest day to be paddling, but we wore wetsuits. I brought the wetsuit that I wore for the Pacific Crest triathlon. It was a skin-tight Orca wetsuit with the Team In Training logo. I felt comfortable in my body and was in the best shape of my life. I was not trying to impress and didn't feel the need to hide from him. I knew he would not take advantage of me.

The day was fun, and I felt good in the stable inflatable kayak, often known as a ducky. Mark paddled his little playboat and was comfortable in it and on his home river. We stopped for lunch at a popular surfing spot. It is a wave where people surf on the river and do other kayak tricks. Few others were on the river that day since it was not officially the in-season for the dam-released river. Two guys were surfing, and Mark knew them both. I sat in the eddy in the ducky, watching as he surfed and talked with the guys. Mark was eager to talk to them and excited to watch them surf. He was no slouch himself, and he surfed like a pro. I watched with a little crooked smile. I thought he was trying to impress me by showing off his skills on the wave. I surfed in the ocean and thought he wanted to show me his surfing skills too.

Now I know that the two guys who were surfing that day were two of the best kayakers on the river, and Mark had a ton of respect for them both. I now have the same respect and love for them and the rest of our river family.

After lunch, we paddled down the rest of the river. I had made it this far unscathed and felt confident in the boating skills I gained in California. I loved being on the whitewater. I remember seeing kayakers on previous raft trips and thinking, *I would never do what they are doing*. I thought they were crazy, and now I was on a date with someone in one of those kayaks.

As we got to a calmer spot, Mark asked me if I wanted to get in his boat and try it. I always loved doing exciting things and jumped at the chance to try them out. So I got into the tiny playboat and paddled some class I rapids while Mark stayed close in the ducky. I did what he told me and made it through successfully. The adrenaline rush was incredible, and I felt comfortable in the boat. He told me later that I was almost burying the nose as I paddled it. At least I was not doing the excessive, reclining Barcalounger posture that we joke about now.

After we got off the river, we drove to a restaurant for dinner closer to home. As we drove in his truck, I felt amazingly comfortable with him. We liked the same music and listened to the radio as we talked. He asked me if he could hold my hand. It felt good to have someone ask permission. He respected me, and I was not a piece of meat to him. My history of sexual assault always haunted me, and I felt safe with Mark. So, I giggled and gave him my hand.

We got to the restaurant and continued to have a comfortable conversation. Mark and I had some friends in common, and I learned about him before we met. These people validated that Mark was a good guy. He even met my sister Lisa and her husband when he spoke at the funeral of a woman who was killed in a car accident. His daughter, son, and ex-wife were in the other car. The woman was like a second mom to my brother-in-law.

This tragedy would forever create a connection between me and Mark's children as I understood their trauma. When someone goes through significant trauma, it changes you, good or bad. One is that a caring adult can help you get through whatever the struggle. I may not have been around when the accident happened, but my experiences could make it safe for them to come to me. I wanted to be that for them if they needed it, and I was not going to push it on them. Mark's daughter Sarah and I have a very special relationship that has continued to grow over the years.

When I mentioned the accident to my sister Lisa, she told me she remembered meeting Mark at the funeral, and they heard him speak to everyone. They were both extremely impressed by his courage, his love for his children, and his faith. As Mark talked about some of these things and other experiences, I felt he was trying to impress me. I told him, "So many people have already told me how great you are. You do not need to try so hard." We joked later that he was dumbfounded, and I shut him up for a minute, which is hard to do. He thought, *she either doesn't care if we have a second date, or she likes me.* It ended up being the second option.

We ended our date with tea back at his house. The entire date was thirteen hours, and it was a fabulous day. He walked me to my car, and I hugged him with a brotherly pat on the back. I wanted to set boundaries in this relationship because I wanted it to go farther than anything else in my life. I did not date for seven years for a reason, and I did not feel worthy of a good relationship. I wanted to ensure that I respected myself, and he respected me too. I was determined not to kiss him on the first date. I wanted to be friends. After all, he was coming to my house for dinner the next day anyway. This adventure on the river was just the beginning of a sixteen-year relationship. We were married after a year and a half of dating.

Our relationship has not always been easy, and the beginning of our marriage was incredibly rocky. I did not realize how traumatized Mark was from his previous two marriages, and that trauma bled over into our marriage. I had done a lot of work on myself, and now it was time for me to heal in a relationship with someone who also needed to heal.

I suspected that Mark had ADHD early on in our relationship, and his behavior affected our relationship. I searched for an adult ADHD self-assessment to see if that would help with the conversation. I started doing the research and found a survey online that identified the key symptoms of ADHD for an adult looking for answers. I found the Adult ADHD Self-Report Scale (ASRS-v1.1) Symptom Checklist a great starting resource. I read the items one by one, intending to share them with Mark for him to complete. I could connect the items to symptoms I observed in Mark, and then it hit me. I thought, *oh crap, this is me!* I have always struggled with wrapping up the final details of projects, remembering appointments, fidgeting, and constantly having some movement with my body, interrupting, and finishing people's sentences, impulse shopping, and making decisions, just to name a few. So how did I miss this? How did my teachers and parents miss this? It was glaringly apparent to me at that moment and explained so much of my life.

I told Mark about my realization. He chuckled with amusement as I told him the details. I also realized that I still needed to focus on healing myself. I needed to be completely honest and ask for help as much as possible. We have a friend who is a psychiatrist, and he suggested that I go to the University of Pennsylvania Adult ADHD Center in Philadelphia. I reached out to them and scheduled a complete psychological evaluation since I had never had a formal one before. I felt confused more than ever. Were my issues PTSD, anxiety, ADHD, or all the above? I could not tell and wanted to ensure I had an accurate diagnosis to get the most effective treatment.

I was excited and nervous about having the evaluation. We had to fill out paperwork in advance. Those close to me also had to complete surveys to get their perspectives on my symptoms. Mark and my oldest sister Paula filled out the surveys. I did not ask my mom because I did not think she would remember some of my symptoms as a child. Mom was in her late eighties, and it did not make sense for me to ask her. Mom was very laid back and had some form of ADHD as well.

Mark and his son Nathan went with me to the in-person evaluation portion. It took an entire day, and they sat in for some of my interviews. I wanted to model being transparent and vulnerable with the hope that it would someday help them process their past traumas. It was a long day, but I felt terrific because I was finally going to get some answers. It took a few weeks, but I went back for the results.

I went to UPenn's Adult ADHD Center on my own this time. Not because I did not want others to hear the results but because they had other commitments. The psychologist who conducted the central part of my evaluation shared the results with me. I had post-traumatic stress disorder (PTSD), attention deficit hyperactivity disorder (ADHD)—the combined type of hyperactive and distracted forms—generalized anxiety disorder (GAD), and social anxiety. I was surprised by the social anxiety, but it made sense as I thought about it. I would avoid situations if I thought I potentially had a panic attack. I was aware of how my panic attacks impacted me and did not want others to see that side of me.

Having an official diagnosis from a full diagnostic assessment was liberating. I now had labels to understand why I had struggled my entire life. I was not ashamed of it. It was a badge of honor that I had survived and, at times, thrived despite these struggles. Things made more sense, and I was ready to dig into whatever I needed to grow from this experience. I shared this information with my family in the hope that they would find freedom for themselves. My story matters, and I can help others heal by sharing my own story of resilience.

> *I forgive myself for buying into the lie that I may never be married and that no one would want me if they knew the real me. I thought that I was damaged and beyond repair. The truth is that I have a lot to offer someone in a relationship, and I am a blessing to my husband and the family I have gained through him. Just because I went through significant adversities does not mean I was or am broken. The healing process I went through can serve as a model to help others and has only strengthened me.*

Chapter 13

Taking My Healing from Self to Others

The work I had done on myself was just the beginning. God had other plans for me—to take my story of trauma and healing to help others heal. Once I had gotten through some intensive therapy, I was ready to go to the next level of therapy. I received cognitive behavior therapy, imago therapy, and other modalities of talk therapy that gave me a breadth of skills for managing my emotional pain.

I learned to set boundaries when others directed their emotions at me, and I became more comfortable having difficult conversations. I still struggled with this since I spent most of my life accepting whatever people said about me, especially the harmful stuff. I had listened to the lies, which seeped into all aspects of my life. The negative beliefs about myself were not all gone, but my identity was rooted much more in my identity through Jesus. He touched my heart in a way that helped change my thoughts and beliefs about myself if I listened to what He thought of me and not others' thoughts and beliefs.

Mark and I had a few rough patches early in our marriage, and we found a counselor of his choosing. A friend recommended Dominic Herbst and his Restoring Relationships model of counseling. It was a Christian counseling model that focused on healing past traumas and understanding how they impacted us in our current relationships. It was life changing.

Dominic is a man's man, as Mark called him. Dominic and Mark connected as men of God, and Dominic helped Mark feel safe to express some of his deepest hurts. We both had to do some challenging work and process the hurt others caused us. This process finally released both Mark and me from a lot of unresolved trauma.

Our counseling with Dominic was a significant turning point for us both. I knew I had healed alone but healing in a relationship was the test of coming out of the fire of lies. God had taken me from being a wounded bird to a phoenix rising from the ashes. I was finally a person who had something to offer others, and I did not need to hide my pain. I had become stronger because of the pain and past adversities. God wanted me to be a model of his grace and healing by sharing my story with others to give them hope. He led me to become a special education teacher and Board-Certified Behavior Analyst, so I could understand myself better and help others. I loved working with children with special needs as I understood them and what they were going through. I did not understand what I was going through as a child, but I can look back and recognize what helped and hurt me. I also understand my family much more and acknowledge that they all went through traumas too. They did the best they could with what they had.

After working with Dominic, I was ready to dig into the last pieces of trauma that still impacted me. One major piece of the healing puzzle for me was Eye Movement Desensitization and Reprocessing (EMDR) therapy, a treatment to help our brains re-process distressing experiences that were previously processed inadequately. The dysfunctional coping skills, thoughts, beliefs, and attitudes I had developed due to the childhood traumas were not helpful for me. I wanted to dig deep into the pain to break free from it finally. I went to a psychologist who was a certified EMDR therapist. I made incredible strides very quickly.

One session was especially memorable and meaningful for me. The time I spent in the hospital as a four-year-old girl after the car accident has had a hold on childhood memories throughout my life. After fifty-two years, I can still picture the hospital room in my head. The smells, sights, sounds and feelings have haunted me for most of my life. My therapist had me visualize the hospital room and think of the emotions, self-talk, and physical responses I experienced from this memory. I put on the headphones with soothing ocean sounds playing as part of the EMDR therapy. I closed my eyes and focused on the hospital room. I could see the stark white walls and floors, the windows with bars blocking them, and the cribs each of us slept in. I was reminded of waking up to a needle in my butt every morning and the little red wagon they used to distract us from our family's departure after visiting hours ended.

As I settled into these thoughts and experiences, I prayed for God to be with me through this process. Immediately after meditating to ask God to carry me, the vision of the hospital changed. I could see a light in the window that I hadn't seen before. I felt my little body gently flying out of the crib and pushing the window open with the bars falling away. I saw myself flying out the window and over a beach with ocean waves washing up on the sand. As I flew over the beach, I could see handwriting in the sand, though I couldn't make out what it said. As the surf washed over the writing in the sand, the writing disappeared once the water drained back into the ocean. I felt God saying this writing represented the pain that continued to be carried in my body and brain. He was washing it away through the process of EMDR, and my willingness to give it all up to Him working together. God used EMDR to break the chains of trauma as long as I was willing to let it go.

As I shared this entire experience as it was happening in the counselor's office, I was describing to him how my body, emotions, and thoughts of myself were breaking free from the damage caused by the trauma of that specific memory. I narrated the entire experience to him as he intently listened to me. The vision of the hospital room suddenly had less of a grip on my emotions. In fact, I now experienced joy when I pictured the room, as I felt the freedom to open the window and fly out to escape the terrible memories that gripped me for so long. I cried tears of joy at these new experiences and thoughts.

My counselor was astonished by what I told him. He used a pain scale rating between zero and ten—ten being the highest level of emotional pain and zero being the lowest. This memory previously caused me pain around the level of seven or eight. After that one session, the pain I experienced was only about level two. Now, not only is my pain level almost zero, but I also experience joy thinking about opening the window in the hospital room and flying out. It's an incredible process that I continued through other painful experiences in the following months and years. I stopped EMDR therapy after there were no longer past experiences that had a grip on me as they did before. I tell anyone who still suffers from previous trauma to consider trying EMDR; perhaps they'll find it as effective as I did.

> *I forgive myself for buying into the lies that the trauma I experienced as a child will always impact me significantly. The truth is that I have found strength and freedom from receiving treatment and digging into the pain rather than running away from it. It has been a process that has been easier because of God's help and the professional help of several different counselors over the years. There is not one way to heal, and everyone has their own path to follow. My path has given me*

hope and belief in miracles that strengthen me daily. I would not change a thing I have experienced.

Chapter 14

Freedom in Facing New Challenges

As I author this book, I am blessed with an incredible husband, stepchildren, and four granddaughters, with a grandson on the way. I have helped our family to give our granddaughters the skills to talk about things that bother them, make it safe for us to process our pain and disappointments, and build resilience to bounce back from challenges. Mark and I have developed an open-book policy on our struggles as individuals and as a couple. We are stronger now than we've ever been, and we share our journey with transparency and vulnerability with a goal to help others experiencing similar things.

I pursued my doctorate in educational psychology and graduated from West Virginia University in 2021. I have continued to be a lifelong learner, figuring myself out and sharing my lessons learned with others in my sphere of influence. For example, I now have a company providing consulting and coaching services to school districts to create safe, supportive, and trauma-sensitive schools and other human services organizations in Pennsylvania and across the country. I advocate for our family and other families who struggle with trauma, mental illness, substance use disorders, and co-occurring disorders for all populations.

> *I forgive myself for buying into the lie that I should be seen and not heard. The truth is that I need to trust my intuition and wherever it takes me. My story is one of triumph over trauma, and I need to continue sharing my gifts of learning, healing, and empowerment. My voice gives strength to others when I am vulnerable and present.*

Chapter 15

What Would I Say to My Younger Self?

You are perfect, just the way you are, scars and all. You spent most of your life trying to fit in and acting like what you were feeling on the inside was not real. You had so much to offer, and you hid it because you thought that your story did not matter and that something was wrong with you. It was not about what was wrong with you but what happened to you. The trauma was real and impacted you in ways you may never fully understand. That is okay. You do not have to fix every little thing you do not see as perfect. What you have been through has made you stronger than you imagined. So, give yourself grace, and remember that your scars do not define you.

The people around you, including your family, did their best with what they knew how to do. They may not have always supported you the way you needed it, but they hurt for you too. What you suffered was horrible for anyone to go through. You do not have to be strong and suck it up to get past this. God will carry you through the pain if you let Him. Others will admire you when you share your weaknesses and be vulnerable. You are not a bad person, so do not believe lies that the voice inside your head tells you to break you down.

Your strength will become an essential part of your personality, and the traumas helped to build that strength. Remember, you do not have to be strong for yourself and everyone else. Enjoy the blessings and struggles that you will experience. You have a right and a duty to set boundaries for yourself as self-care. It is not selfish to take care of your needs. When you fill yourself up, you will have more to give others. Otherwise, you will pour from an empty cup with a full plate of overwhelm and responsibilities. This empty cup will not serve you or those you want to help. So put your oxygen mask on first. I love you just the way you are!

Signed,
Your future self

Society teaches us to let go of the past if it is not related to the present time. We are encouraged to suck it up and move on. People say they went through many terrible things in their life and turned out fine. Really? I hope they are right. I know for me, I said these same things, and I was really saying it to cover up the pain and struggles. It was too difficult for me to look at it at the time, but ignoring it never made it go away. It was a false sense of security that only added more fuel to the fire of my struggles.

Society as a whole has always been numb to traumas, and so many people continue to suffer silently. The events of the past twenty-one years since the turn of the century have opened wounds for our world that have been covered up by complacency. The wounds have been there festering, and now they are open for all to see. COVID-19 offered us a positive aspect, as it forced all of us to look at what matters most in our lives. We cannot continue the path that allows hurt people to hurt others. We are in the middle of a mental health crisis in our country that will continue to spiral and expand unless we do something about it. Even when our country is more divided than I have seen it in my lifetime, I continue to be hopeful and look for ways to inspire people to be vulnerable with each other. When we choose to be vulnerable, we will find that digging into the pain will reveal strength, beauty, and healing. Paraphrasing Matthew 22:36-40, I try to remember that I must "Love God, and love others as myself." My life's goal is to live this out in everything I do, and I know that I will be successful, loved, and blessed.

> *I forgive myself for buying into the lie that I must have done something to deserve all the pain and adversity that has happened to me. The truth is that so much of the trauma is what happened to me and not something that is wrong with me. Every time we bounce back from the darkness, the light gets brighter and brighter.*

Epilogue

Yet Another Trauma

On the evening of November 19, 2019, I received a phone call from Mark's dad, Bob. He and I have a great relationship, but his call seemed to be unexpected. He asked, "So, where are you working these days?" I was working from home that day, but normally I traveled a lot for my work. He was very calm and even mannered, as he usually is. He proceeded to tell me that Mark had an accident and fell off a roof. He said the hospital tried calling me but couldn't reach me, even though my phone was sitting beside me. It was probably better that Bob called me because I probably would have freaked out if the hospital had called me. Bob softened the blow of this horrible news.

Mark was alive, and they had him at the emergency room at Geisinger Medical Center, only fifteen minutes from home. I called my two sisters and told them and quickly grabbed my purse to head to the hospital. I called Mark's two children as I drove to the hospital. I didn't know much at this point, so I could be calm overall. In my head, I thought that Mark had fallen from about ten feet and maybe he had a broken arm or leg. Mark's dad was at the hospital when I got there, and we waited for the doctor to come and talk to us. They gave us bits and pieces of information as they were still working to stabilize Mark. One thing I could cling to was that the trauma doctor said, "Mark was fully conscious and talking when they brought him into the ER." That made me feel much better. Little did I know what lay ahead of Mark and our family.

Mark fell thirty feet. He had seven fractured vertebrae, with two of them burst, sixteen displaced fractured ribs, a broken clavicle, collapsed lungs, and a slice in his sub-clavicular artery that feeds blood to the brain. He lost over half of the blood from his body and they had him intubated. They finally let us see him after taking three hours to stabilize him. Mark's dad, his son Nathan and I visited him in a special ER section reserved for serious traumas. Sarah lives five hours away and could not get there that first night.

As we walked closer to him, we saw blood on the floor and tubes coming from almost every opening in his body, including two chest tubes and IVs. He was conscious but very groggy. The first thing he mouthed to me when he saw me was, "I'm sorry." We've been through so much together, and he felt bad adding more to my plate. I was simply happy he was alive! I knew it was simply an uncontrolled accident because he was *always* safe when working.

This night began another long and challenging journey for our family, then COVID-19 hit. Mark and I are authoring another book about his accident and all the miracles and challenges surrounding the accident. You will have to get that book to hear about his difficult yet amazing recovery and the miraculous story of faith, hope, strength, trust, healing, and resilience. The book will be called *Grace, Grief, and Gravity*. I hope you join us for this next chapter of our journey. Blessings to you.

Acknowledgements

Thank you to my husband Mark for always believing in me and supporting me to go bigger! You are my biggest cheerleader, even when you are a "recovering pusher"! I love you!

Thank you to my family, especially my big sister Paula for being a part of this trauma journey from the very beginning, and for reading my draft before anyone else to give me your honest feedback. Thank you to my sister Lisa for your support of my journey to healing in many ways.

Thank you to the rest of my siblings and family for engaging me in sometimes painful discussions as I explored my past.

Thank you to my incredible stepchildren Sarah and Nathan, and their families. I love you as if you were my own blood!

To all our grandchildren-Emily, Claire, Sophina, Elana, and Ronan. This book is for you, so you don't have to go through what I have gone through.

Finally, this book is dedicated to my mom and dad. I wish you were both here to share this with me. I love and miss you both very much!

References

Shapiro, F. M. (2002). Eye movement desensitization and reprocessing (EMDR): Information processing in the treatment of trauma. *Journal of clinical psychology, 58*(8), 933-946.

Turnbull, G. (1998, March). A review of post-traumatic stress disorder. Part I: Historical development and classification. *Injury, 29*(2), 87-91.

Webb, J. (2012). *Running on empty: Overcome your childhood emotional neglect.* Morgan James Publishing.

Wikipedia Contributors. (2022, September 18). *Where the Heart Is (2000 film).* Retrieved October 14, 2022, from Wikipedia, The Free Encyclopedia: https://en.wikipedia.org/w/index.php?title=Where_the_Heart_Is_(2000_film)&oldid=1110871651